The Achievement Trap

The Over-Achiever, People-Pleaser, & Perfectionist's Guide to Freedom & True Success

By Brandilyn Tebo

The Achievement Trap

Published by B. C. Allen Publishing and Tonic Books

1500 SE Hawthorne Blvd.
Portland, OR 97214
Now taking manuscript submissions and book ideas at any stage of the process.
submissions@tonicbooks.online

Printed in the United States of America

First Printing, 2018

ISBN: 978-0-9968551-7-4

Brandilyn Tebo
www.brandilyntebo.com

Condition:

Stuck in The Achievement Trap

Symptoms:

- Frequently feels stressed, anxious, uncertain, ashamed and/or fearful.
- Panics whenever she feels she is not getting enough done.
- Gives much significance to others' opinions of her.
- Constantly feels that she and/or her work isn't done, isn't ready or isn't good enough.
- Judges her worth based on how busy she is.
- Feels inadequate despite accomplishments.
- Needs to make sure everyone around her is happy before she can be.
- Dwells on whether or not she is "doing it right" in her work, health, relationships, and creative projects.
- Looks outside of herself for validation of her own choices, preferences, attitudes, desires and beliefs.
- Seeks permission from others to be herself and follow her heart.

- Needs to know that other people approve of her before she can approve of herself.
- Self-quantifies (looks to numbers, like her weight, salary, or Instagram followers to measure her worth).
- Doubts her ability to contribute to the world.
- Feels that she needs to prove herself/earn the right before really going after her dreams.

Table of Contents

Foreword

There is a lie in our society and it's killing us. The lie is "When something happens, I will be happy." Notice how many times a day you think it. We live in a constant state of believing that when we finally date the person, leave the job, get divorced, make money, sell the house, get the car, have a drink, etc. we will finally be happy. Even as you read this, you might look ahead to see how long the foreword is, because you might be tricking yourself again with the idea that when you finish it, you will be happy. We feel this lie, yet we have a mountain of evidence from our past that can remind us of the many times we did achieve something and immediately thought "What's next?"

I am grateful enough that I was able to attain many of my childhood dreams. I got to be a professional standup comedian, act in hit movies, date amazing people, and make good money doing what I love. The ironic twist is that I was becoming more and more depressed with each achievement. The more I got what I wanted, the more stressed I became. It was almost as if just by believing that these accomplishments were the source of my happiness,

I felt a responsibility to make sure that they never fell apart. After all, these accomplishments were now my identity and if I lost them, I would be nothing. I worked harder and harder to achieve more, while not enjoying anything that I had. I was exhausted. It might have been a dream, but I was truly miserable.

We all agree that drugs, alcohol, porn, cigarettes etc. are all different types of addictions. But very few people talk about the fact that the constant need for achievement is one of the most common and most subtle addictions that we have as a collective.

At one point I realized this, and I just let go.

The day that I stopped trying to be somewhere else was the day that I truly started living. I learned I was enough. I learned that things were ok. I learned that I don't have to seek approval to be happy. I learned that I don't have to be better than anyone else. I could be what I wanted to be. I could be me.

My big switch was to leave the old belief and replace it with "When I am happy, things will happen." My new job was to be ok with myself, no matter what.

As I became ok with myself and all of my emotions, I started feeling true fulfillment. I discovered there is no "over there" to seek and I only have this moment. What a relief.

Oddly, the more I am just ok with myself, the more things just kind of happen. As we become more centered, we become safe for others. As you connect with your heart, people just want to be around you. The happier you are, the more creative you become. What I am saying is this: When you stop trying to achieve everything, more things happen.

There are incredible things trying to happen for you. You just have to get out of your own way and let them happen.

No flower achieves blooming. No dog tries to bark. No sun uses strenuous effort to shine. They are just BEING what they naturally are. We have our own unique, and powerful abilities on the other side of our addiction to achieve the constant desires of the ego. Your heart will do a better job.

Brandilyn Tebo told me what her book was about and I got really happy. I was happy that more people will learn how to take it easy on themselves. I am excited about the idea that she is going to offer her deepest truth to the world and that she will help people unhook from their own "Achievement Trap." Brandilyn is doing an incredible job at discovering her truth and she is doing the REAL WORK.

It's hard to face your own shit. It's rare to find a person who is willing to do it. That's a reason why Brandilyn is a hero of mine. She is the real thing and has a lot to share. Take your time reading this book. You have nowhere else to be.

I know that by giving us this gift, she is expanding the role of consciousness, and getting us all a little closer to the truth of who we really are.

Enjoy.

Kyle Cease

Preface

It was 4am. I was the only one left in the quiet section of my college library. I had been staring at my computer screen for 10 hours.

My eyes were so dry that my contacts had begun to harden.

I was reading my essay titled "Hierarchies of Power and the Justification of Violence" over for the 12th time.

It has got to be perfect, I thought to myself.

I have gotten straight A's since third grade, I can't mess up now.

Working on my paper was pushed to the last minute because after class on Monday and Tuesday that week, I worked my job at the Farmer's Market.

On Wednesday, after my classes, I hosted a dinner party for my animal activist club.

I had flown from Los Angeles to San Francisco for a modeling job on Friday and Saturday.

And as always, I had visited the office hours of each of my professors that week to ask clarifying questions about the material. And worked out at the gym every day.

I hadn't had any other time to write the essay, but t*here are no excuses for imperfection,* I thought.

My body was exhausted, but I was numb to that fact.

Lack of sustenance, sleep, and self-compassion left me feeling like a zombie.

I numbed my burn-out with my addictions to busyness, stress, hunger, exercise, and most of all: external validation.

As I strained to find any last typos or redundancies I might have missed, my stomach grumbled audibly.

I hadn't eaten since 6pm because I didn't want to exceed my calories for the day.

I was already severely underweight, but to me, I was never thin *enough.*

Likewise, I got straight A's, the praise of my professors and leadership awards, but I never felt accomplished *enough.*

All of my accomplishments were invisible to me, because all I could see was where I was lacking.

I didn't know it then, but I was stuck deep down in The Achievement Trap.

I was constantly stressed about how I needed to achieve more and be better.

Being stressed out about how much I needed to do was weirdly comforting.

Subconsciously, I believed that if I wasn't stressed out—if I wasn't being as productive as humanly possible—that I would lose my value, and therefore be unlovable.

I was terrified of others thinking that I wasn't busy enough, accomplished enough, good enough. To my ego, being seen as lazy, weak, or a failure was death.

A full to-do list was my safety blanket. The more overwhelmed I felt, the safer I felt.

I not only had an eating disorder, but also a "doing" disorder, which centered around the belief "having free time means I'm wasting my potential."

I used my weight and my accomplishments to quantify my worth.

I was imprisoned by my own mind.

My thoughts had become a broken record, playing the questions "am I doing enough?" "am I doing it right?" "am I good enough?" maddeningly on repeat.

I now see that being stuck in the Achievement Trap is like Sisyphus being damned to an eternity of unending hard work in a futile quest for validation.

Each day, we roll the metaphorical boulder of proving our worth up a steep hill. For a split second after an accomplishment, we can proclaim that we have done enough! But a moment later, we watch it roll back down to the bottom as that accomplishment becomes meaningless. We begin the quest of proving ourselves all over again.

We've gotten so caught up in the need to prove ourselves that we prevent ourselves from really having a life we love. We took away our own permission to fully enjoy life. We think that we'll be allowed to feel how we want to feel once we just achieve that one… more… goal.

This is the Achievement Trap. And my guess is that, if you're reading this book, you're stuck in it.

But there's hope. You no longer have to live your life feeling unfulfilled, chasing achievements that you think will complete you. It is possible to have goals that truly inspire you and that are a form of your true self-expression rather than goals that feel like stressful obligations.

Paradoxically, when you are no longer dependent on achievements for your self-worth, you actually achieve at a greater rate. When you drop the stress, your achievements are more meaningful and fulfilling. You're more creative, curious, and disciplined because your work is coming from a greater space of joy. You have more will power. You get exactly what you want quicker than you've ever gotten it.

For more videos about my personal story, visit the *online resource guide.*

Here's what to expect

This book will walk you through how to, step by step, create goals that are truly inspiring. It will give you access to discovering what you really want out of life, and the knowledge that you deserve it.

For example, a coaching client of mine had been trying to slim down for years before we started working together. Weight loss was her #1 life goal. She thought that once she lost the weight, she would finally feel confident, comfortable in her body, excited about life, and able to be vulnerable with her partner.

She put her life on pause until she lost the weight. She got excited on the days when she was a few pounds lighter, but overall, she felt constantly stressed and disappointed in herself. It was hard for her to focus on the things that really mattered to her. She was a painter but had stopped creating her art. She used to love going on hiking adventures with her partner, but never felt like leaving the house much anymore.

After I walked her through the process that I'm about to show you, she realized that her weight loss goal (not the weight itself) was what was preventing her from having the life she wanted.

Rather than needing a number on the scale to prove her worth, she actually dug down to the source of her feelings of unworthiness and dealt with them head on.

This freed her up to live her life from a place of inspiration, not shame. She felt more confident and healthier than ever and gave herself permission to be vulnerable with her partner regardless of her weight. She started creating her art and going on adventures again. She realized that the weight was irrelevant to her happiness, and her body was able to find its own healthiest weight.

The material in this book worked for her and so many others—and it will work for you too.

This book is designed to help you identify which of your goals have their roots in feelings of unworthiness, and replace them with heart-based goals rooted in the knowledge that you are enough.

You no longer have to be the person who gets stuck living your life from accomplishment to accomplishment, without being truly present and enjoying your life. If you commit to doing the exercises in this book as designed, you can free yourself from the Achievement Trap.

But first, a word of caution: you have likely invested a lot of mental energy in the belief that you need your accomplishments to prove your worth, like I did. Your ego-identity has constructed itself around your accomplishments, and thinks that it needs them in order to survive. So if you experience yourself wanting to walk away from this book (even though you know you're stuck in the Achievement Trap), that might just be your ego's desire to protect itself.

If you do put this book down, it is likely that you will continue to be constrained by an underlying sense of unworthiness and be imprisoned by goals that don't fulfill you. You won't be able to freely give your gifts to the world because you'll be too busy trying to hide the "fact" that you're not good enough.

If you do commit to this book, however, my promise to you is that you will find newfound freedom from dependency on your achievements. You will begin to experience yourself as greater than the sum of your accomplishments. Your identity will no longer be wrapped up in others' opinions of you or your salary, weight, job title, accolades, or social media following. This does not mean that you will stop achieving, it just means that you'll be free from the need for superficial achievements and you'll start creating goals that are truly inspiring and fulfilling.

So before we dive in deep, I want you to make a commitment to yourself. I want you to commit to finishing the book and doing all the exercises *as designed*—even when it feels scary, unnecessary, or uncomfortable. You completing this workbook as designed is the only way that I guarantee that you'll have the freedom we've been talking about.

Deal?

Great. Let's begin.

How'd I get stuck in Here?

Here's the quick and dirty on how we get ourselves stuck in the Achievement Trap.[1]

We start out as shameless, unapologetic, excited, DGAF little kids who sense that anything is possible (remember the good old days?). But then—WHAM!—we have our first experience of failure: we're not picked for soccer, a parent walks out, we face abuse, our crush turns us down, friends laugh at us... In response to this, we subconsciously decide that because we failed to stay safe or get love or belonging or approval, it must mean that we are fundamentally not good enough.

This is what I call an ego-protective decision. The mind sees failure as a virus that it needs to protect itself from. So, like the immune system produces antibodies to protect the body from sickness, the mind produces limiting beliefs that it thinks will protect the ego from future failures.

---

1. Watch the video of me explaining this on the online resource guide. See page 132 for the URL

For example, in third grade math class, I was called up to the board to do the problem 27 divided by three using long division. Being up in front of everyone caused me to have a total brain fart and I multiplied rather than divided. Some of the cool kids in the class started laughing and the hot fire of embarrassment spread across my face and down my neck as I went back to my seat.

In that moment, I decided that I am bad at math. My subconscious made this decision in an attempt to protect me from future embarrassment, rejection, or failure. That summer, when it came time to sign up for classes the following year, I put myself in advanced everything... besides math.

I spent the rest of my years in school needing to over achieve in every other subject to compensate for my perceived mathematical stupidity. Although I wasn't aware of it at the time, that third grade decision became a self-fulfilling prophecy which profoundly shaped my life.

Because protective decisions are subconscious, limiting beliefs fester under the surface, undetected. They make us exert lots of time and energy in a futile attempt to compensate for our perceived inadequacies. We think that once we sufficiently prove ourselves, we will be immune from being hurt, like we were in the past. Our achievements then become a smoke screen, blocking our feelings of inadequacy from our view.

These feelings of not-enough-ness parade around as ambition/determination. But really they're a masked attempt to prove our worthiness. Often, people who are "goal-oriented" have deep rooted feelings of inadequacy. Our goals allow us to live in the future and prevent us from actually having to deal with the feelings of unworthiness in the present moment. We get so caught up in goal achievement that we are (conveniently) distracted from having to confront our underlying feelings.

The problem is that we set these goals under the false assumption that once they're achieved, our underlying feelings of inadequacy will disappear. We think that achievements equal feeling good about ourselves. And they do! But only for a short time. When we accomplish something, our brain releases endorphins which cause a momentary high, just like a drug.

This high does not heal our insecurities nor help us to know our own intrinsic worth. When we achieve in order to feel good about ourselves, we become dependent upon achievements like a drug addict. We lose the ability to feel good without them.

Trying to cover up the parts of ourselves that we don't like with accomplishments is like drinking salt water to quench our thirst. The more we drink, the thirstier we are.

Likewise, the more we accomplish, the more we *need* to accomplish to distract ourselves from feeling not good enough, and the cycle continues. It's a loop that just keeps feeding back into itself. We feel trapped. Exhausted. Uninspired.

When we actually achieve a goal, we may feel good about ourselves for a brief time, but eventually, the same uncomfortable feeling that caused us to set the goal in the first place resurfaces. Achieving to compensate for feeling unworthy is like putting icing on top of a pile of mud and calling it dessert. Our core beliefs about ourselves remain, despite how great our lives look. Eventually, the feelings of unworthiness emerge.

We shouldn't achieve in order to feel good about ourselves. Really it should be the other way around. We should feel good about ourselves first, then achieve from that good-feeling place.

The canvas of your life

Think of it this way: you start out life with a blank canvas—you can paint whatever you want on it!

The opportunities are endless! But then, over time, each rejection, failure, hurt, abandonment, disappointment, failure, and betrayal puts a little smear on our canvas, clouding up your space to create.

Now, as we stand and look at our canvas, it doesn't seem like we can paint whatever we want. It seems like we have to work around the dried-up splotches and smears that are already there. Whatever we decide to paint is constrained by all the smudges from our past. It's not what we would have painted if we had a white canvas and could paint anything. Trying to paint on a smudged-up yucky canvas is silly.

Setting goals from a place of "I'm not enough and now I have to achieve in order to hide that I'm not enough" is just as silly. We need to clean up our canvas so that we can again create anything we want.

Losing weight, earning money, gaining followers, getting promoted, or running marathons will not help us to clean up our canvas. The sense of unworthiness will remain. We just have painted over what's there, not actually making something new, but simply trying to correct or hide what's underneath.

We will only run ourselves into the ground believing that if we just achieve a little bit more, we'll finally prove that we're good enough (enter: workaholism, compulsive exercise, eating disorders, perfectionism, drug addictions—you name it).

The good news is that we can start at our goals and work backwards until we get to the source of them. Our goals can grant us direct access to healing our sense of unworthiness.

We're about to begin the work of getting you back to a blank canvas—back to the place where you are free to create goals that are worthy of your life.

So if you think that healing your dependency on achievements is going to turn your life into a mess—I totally get you!

Your Dirty Little Secret

When I was a little girl, I was excited by everything and totally unafraid of making a fool of myself or failing. I never felt the need to prove myself. I only did things that really inspired me.

I wrote poems and dramatically read them to my class. I wore an Ariel costume under all of my clothes and called myself an undercover mermaid. I created mudslides in the pouring rain. I started a "restaurant" in our garage and sold saltine crackers for $1 a piece. I put on dance performances at family gatherings. I had zero concerns about what other people thought of me. I thought I could do no wrong.

But then one day, when I was seven, something happened to me that changed all of that. I was sexually assaulted by an older boy.

I decided "I'm bad," (one of those protective decisions that we talked about earlier).

I thought that I would never feel clean or good again.

I thought that there must have been a part of me that wanted it to happen. Some sick, gross, dirty, bad, wrong part of me.

The next thirteen years of my life were consumed by my trying to compensate for feeling dirty and not good enough.

I didn't want anyone to know that I was secretly a bad girl, so I did everything in my power to be good. In middle school, sometimes I slept only a few hours a night to make sure that I got perfect scores on my exams.

On top of being a straight-A student, I was in the school plays, competed in science fairs and cheerleading competitions, sat on the student council, and did community service.

But I still didn't feel clean. I still didn't feel good enough. I was still afraid that others would find out how secretly bad I was.

In high school, I was in all honors classes and still got straight A's. I held leadership positions in four different clubs. I was captain on the debate team. I volunteered, taught classes, started my own tutoring business, wrote for the school paper, went vegan, and became an animal activist.

Still not good enough.

Towards the end of high school, I started modeling. The industry promised me that I could be world-renowned for my beauty. I thought that this, if true, would finally make me feel good enough.

Soon, my need to prove my worth extended beyond just grades, extracurricular activities and accomplishments. I looked at my body and thought that any fat that I had might reveal to others that I actually wasn't good enough.

I thought it might betray to the outside world that I was actually bad and gross.

So I started dieting. To feel clean again. To prove my worth. To hide the "bad" part of me.

One day, after leaving a casting where the models were rail-thin, I went to the bathroom and saw how my thighs spread out over the toilet seat. "Still not thin enough," I thought. I pulled up my shirt and saw how my stomach rolled when I bent over. "Not good enough," I thought.

The refrains from my childhood echoed hauntingly again: I need to be good. I need to be clean.

I was already restricting myself. The thought that I would have to restrict myself even more to feel good enough was maddening. I felt desperate. I cried and hyperventilated in the bathroom stall. And from then on, I ate less.

I'd frequently check the back of my thighs in the mirror. If I saw dimples, I'd eat even less. I'd bend over. If my skin rolled, I'd eat even less. I could no longer connect with others or enjoy experiences because I was constantly in my head, analyzing how many calories I took in and burned.

I was diagnosed with anorexia. The modeling industry told me I looked great. My doctor told me my body had begun to eat away at my liver.

I ate less and less but never felt cleaner, stronger, or better.

I dieted in order to numb myself from the feeling of being bad that crept in whenever I wasn't achieving. The emotional hunger I suppressed was so much greater than my hunger for food. I also suppressed my cravings for nurturing, self-acceptance, pleasure, vulnerability, connection, and relaxation. I felt that I was wrong to want these things.

I associated these desires with the "bad" part of me that must have deserved my assault. The part of me that I was afraid would take over if I stopped achieving for a second. So I only allowed myself to want what I thought I should want: to be productive, high-achieving, and disciplined.

As I shared about in the opening of this book, the restrictive eating, the straight A's and the over-involvement persisted in college. On top of modeling and working two part-time jobs, I founded and ran a farm animal activism club that won "Organization of the Year." I got a leadership service award. I held weekly community dinners. I hosted activist conferences. I worked out almost every day. I didn't drink or party. I was so "good."

I felt that if I slowed down, let up, or released some control, that the floodgates would open. I feared that others would finally figure out that I'm actually just a bad, wrong, gross little girl.

One day, after eating a big muffin, I was feeling particularly disgusted with myself. I thought I could feel the calories turning into fat on my body. I went for a run, wanting to burn away how gross I felt. I wanted to burn away everything that felt dirty and unworthy about me. I wanted to run so hard that my body had to consume every unnecessary bit of flesh on my bones. I was trying to run from my feelings of unworthiness. I was trying to run from myself.

But it wasn't working. I ran harder and harder and I wasn't feeling any better. I started feeling tired and hated myself for being so weak. I ran harder.

I wondered how hard I would need to run to feel good enough. To feel clean. I desperately asked myself, "When will I feel good enough? When is my worthiness going to come back?"

And then, somewhere from the very depths of my being, an answer came: "It's not."

The thought repeated itself with every stride.

"It's not coming back."

"It's not coming back."

"It's not coming back."

I had spent the majority of my life trying to achieve enough that I would feel worthy, but my worthiness wasn't going to come back.

This dawning realization made me stop right where I was, in the middle of the park near my house, panting from the run. I melted into a heap of sobs on the grass.

I had achieved everything that I had set out to achieve, yet I didn't feel any better about myself.

And I suddenly understood. *My worthiness wasn't coming back—because it was never gone.*

I had forbidden myself from everything that I loved about life—relaxation, connection, laughter, joy, spontaneity, fun, nurturing—thinking that if I just achieved enough, that one day I would earn the right to love myself again.

But I had never lost the right in the first place. I had it all along.

Years of self-torment came cascading down upon me and, in a flash, I realized how absurd it was that I had been torturing myself all that time.

I realized I had been trying my whole life to repent for being a weak girl and a bad girl, when all I needed to do was love that little girl inside of me who felt so weak and so bad. I didn't need to punish her anymore. I didn't need to destroy her.

I needed to embrace her, accept her, love her, allow her, let her be seen.

And in that moment, with that realization, I became free. I realized that I had been worthy all along, and that there was nothing left to prove. I realized that I deserved to feel good and do what I love.

And out of that moment of clarity—and the subsequent years of therapy, healing, research, meditation, life coaching, and self-development work that followed—this book was written.

Now, I'm no longer concerned with proving myself. I'm a full-time entrepreneur, and I spend my time doing what I love. I'm a transformational coach who helps people fulfill their passions, and lead impactful lives that they love. I host workshops and healing retreats and spend lots of time traveling, dancing, doing yoga, writing poetry, and swimming in the ocean. It's hard for me to distinguish between my work and my play, for they are one in the same.

I wrote this book as a reminder to myself to give love to the little girl inside of me who sometimes feels like she's not enough. The more I wrote, the more I realized that it was for me to hear.

I also wrote this book for you. To help you heal the part of yourself that still believes that you need to work hard and punish yourself in order to be worthy. To remind you that your worthiness is not dependent on what you achieve—it's a birthright.

And to give you access to discovering what you will do with your precious life when you stop running from yourself and give yourself permission to love exactly who you are.

You Will Never Be Good Enough

When I was in the thick of my own Achievement Trap, I would have slapped anyone who told me that I needed to "heal from my dependency on achievements and external validation."

"Healing" from my eating disorder and my doing disorder, to me, meant losing my value.

I didn't care about healing—I cared about accumulating achievements, looking good on the outside and impressing others!

I thought that my desperation to achieve was what made me so great!

I really thought that if I stopped needing achievements and validation to feel good, that I would gain massive amounts of weight, go broke and become a lazy slob that watched TV all day.

So if you think that, by helping you heal your dependency on achievements, is going to turn your life into a mess—I totally get you!

I know that you're probably still looking for how to achieve more, because you still think that that's the key to fulfillment, confidence, and making an impact.

And I promise that the opposite is true. Once you no longer need to achieve in order to feel good enough, your inner power will be unleashed. You will feel even more fulfilled and confident and make a way bigger difference in the world.

So let's get one thing straight: this book will not teach you how to be good enough.

This book is not about teaching you anything, in fact.

This book is designed to un-teach you everything that you learned about "being good enough" and remind you of everything you forgot about your own intrinsic worth.

This book will not help you prove your worth. It will deconstruct the very notion that you *have to* prove your worth.

It's okay if you started reading this book because you wanted to learn how to finally *be good enough*. But that is not what you are going to get.

Hang with me, and I promise that you'll get something even better: the incredibly liberating realization that you can never, ever, ever, ever be good enough. You can only discover that you already are, always were and always will be good enough.

You will find that your intrinsic goodness and worth was always there. Even when you hated yourself. Even when you failed. Even when you felt ashamed and miserable. Even when you thought that no one would love you unless you achieved something more.

Your intrinsic goodness and worth was right there with you. Patiently waiting for you to stop trying to earn it. And it's there right now, as you're reading these words.

Do the work in this book and you will realize that you have nothing to prove. And when you have nothing to prove, absolutely anything is possible for you.

It's Not You, It's Your Goals

A few years ago, I started working with a client named Adi. At the time, Adi was a 35 years old woman—a wife, a mother, and a working professional in child welfare.

After her daughter was born, she found herself constantly stressed-out, worrying about her daughter, her job, her marriage, her weight, and her finances. She often laid awake at night, writing to-do lists in her mind. She felt that she was reaching a breaking point and needed help, fast.

On our first call together, I asked her what goals of hers were causing the most stress. She sounded perplexed and replied, "I don't have any goals I'm working towards right now. I just do whatever needs to be done each day."

"But you do!" I replied. "Each action you take during the course of your day—writing a work email, picking up your daughter from school, calling your husband—is the direct result of a goal you have. Your goals themselves are actually the source of your stress, but you can't see that because you're operating on auto-pilot, ruled by goals that are invisible to you."

Adi slowly began to realize that she did have goals—lots of them. She wanted her daughter to be on honor roll so that she could prove to her own parents that she was a good mom, she wanted to get promoted at her job so that she, a woman of color, could prove herself to the white males she worked with, she wanted to keep her house clean so that she could show the babysitter that she had it all together and she wanted to please her husband and stay thin so that he wouldn't leave her, to name a few.

Once she'd identified the goals that were the source of her stress, we could begin re-working those goals.

I then took her through the process in this book and eventually, Adi found herself getting just as much done in her days, but without the stress and anxiety. She felt inspired, not drained by her goals. She replayed happy memories in her mind as she went to bed, rather than writing to-do-lists.

This process will do the same for you, but we can't work with invisible or unconscious goals.

So take a moment to write out a list of all of the goals that you currently have for your life—whether it's to get that promotion, find that partner, get those followers, run that race, lose that weight, write that book—whatever!

Write down goals that are not measurable as well—maybe goals that you don't really even think of as goals but towards which you are consistently working, like "make sure my family is happy," "look beautiful when I go out in public," "keep my house clean and organized," "be a good friend to everyone," "make my boss proud," or "be physically active." Write down anything that you feel you *have* to do.

Now, take a look at each of these goals and ask yourself the following questions for each goal:

1) Do I believe that once I achieve this goal, life will magically be better?
2) Does my goal drain me of energy?
3) Does my goal feel like an obligation?
4) Do I feel frustrated about not achieving my goal, or not achieving it fast enough?
5) Is the pursuit of this goal actually making me less happy in my life?
6) Have I committed to this goal because, somewhere deep down, I feel that I need to prove my worthiness before I am allowed to feel good?
7) Do I feel like I have to accomplish this goal to satisfy others?
8) Do I find myself resorting to numbing behaviors (drinking, compulsive exercise, etc.) in order to work towards this goal?
9) Do I think that achieving this goal will prove that I'm good enough? For example:
   - Wanting to lose weight to prove that you're not lazy or gross.
   - Wanting to make 6-figures to prove that you're not stupid or inadequate.
   - Wanting to run a marathon to prove that you're not weak.

- Wanting 10,000 Instagram followers to prove that you're not a loser.
- Wanting to take care of everyone to prove that you're a good person.

For any of the goals on your list for which you didn't answer "yes" to any of those questions, that's great! That means that's a goal that already resonates with the true you and was not created to compensate for feeling unworthy. Remember those goals for later, but for now, we're going to focus on the goals for which you did answer "yes" to some or all of the above questions.

Now, pick one goal for which you answered "yes" to many of the questions. Pick a goal that feels stressful and does not often inspire you.

This is the goal that we will use to lead you back to the source of your feelings of unworthiness.

The goal I'm working on ______________________.

Great work identifying a problem goal. We'll use that shortly. But first, a story!

Visit the *online resource guide* on page 132 for a printable workbook.

You Can't Have Confidence!

Confession: I had a HUGE crush on an older, popular guy in high school. I knew his schedule by heart and would time it perfectly so I could always pass him in the hallway. Every time I saw him, I got that falling feeling in the bottom of my stomach. But I lamented to my friends that I just didn't "have" the confidence to tell him.

I treated confidence like an allowance that I had to earn, like something of which I had a fixed quantity, like money. As if each of my successes would make a deposit in my metaphorical confidence bank and each failure would result in a withdrawal.

I thought I needed to get more validation from boys before I could earn the right to be confident around my crush. I'd shamelessly flirt with other guys in the hope that their interest in me would deposit enough into my confidence bank account that I could confess my feelings to him.

I interpreted my nervousness around him as a barrier, as something that was stopping me from saying how I really felt.

So I waited for the fear to subside. And waited. But it never did.

He graduated. I never saw him again.

Said boy still has no idea that I used to think (dream—okay, fantasize!) about him on the regular. I was always too afraid that if I got rejected by him, it would deplete whatever remaining stores of confidence I had.

This is because I thought that my successes or failures dictated how much confidence I was allowed.

I literally didn't think that I COULD do something as bold as ask out an older, popular boy. I thought something like that would take earning more confidence than I possessed.

But what I've learned is that we don't need to earn the right to be confident (or any other way of being). We don't need accomplishments to barter for the ways we want to feel.

We didn't inherit a fixed amount of confidence, nor do we need to save up a certain amount of confidence before we can do things that scare us. That's because confidence isn't something that we "have" at all.

If we X-rayed our bodies, we wouldn't find confidence anywhere!

When someone proclaims "I am confident," it's not because she's some rare breed of human with extra confidence molecules in her blood; it's because she chooses to take bold actions regardless of her doubts and fears.

Confidence is not a possession or an allowance—it is a way of being that we can choose.

Ways of being are not dependent upon how much money we make or what car we drive or how our bodies look or how successful we are or who we are dating.

When we realize that who we want to be is a moment-to-moment choice, we gain the power to be the fullest expression of ourselves regardless of what we've achieved. This frees us from our dependency on achievement, enabling us to be who we want to be regardless of circumstances.

Since I now know that my confidence is not condition-dependent, I am free to be bold even when I know I might fail. I know that confidence is a choice that can't be revoked by failure. I know that I have the right to be confident even if I've failed over and over and over and over again.

So, paradoxically, the best way to have confidence is to realize that we never had it in the first place! We don't have to earn the right to be confident—we choose it.

Being confident—like being a leader, being loving, being connected, being generous, being vulnerable, being proud, being powerful, being trusting, being supportive, being strong, being inspired—is independent of conditions.

Often, we are deluded into thinking that we need to achieve something in order to feel how we want to feel. But then we get so caught up in achieving that we lose sight of what we really wanted in the first place! We think that how we feel is a result of what we have, rather than what way we are being.

But truthfully, we don't need to be rich to be generous. We don't need accolades to be proud. We don't need to lose weight to accept ourselves. We don't need a high-level position to be a leader. We don't need any of these things in order to be happy.

We're never happy because we *have* fame, money, or good looks. These are not causes of happiness. Being happy is the only cause of happiness. Happiness causes itself.

It is an illusion that we need to have certain things in order to be a certain way.

Luckily, we don't actually need to exchange our accomplishments for permission to be confident, happy, loving, connected, or peaceful.

Now you try!

This section will help you find the shortcut to getting what you really want. Rather than having to earn a master's degree, lose 100 pounds, or be employee of the month, you can cut to the chase and start being how you want to be and feeling how you want to feel. You can work towards goals from a place of inspiration rather than achievement dependency.

Below is a chart that will help you be who you want to be, independent of the validation of others. On the left is a list of things you may feel that you are missing or things you think you need more of before you can be who you want to be. Although it seems like you are lacking these things, in reality, you don't need anything from anyone in order to be who you want to be. On the right are suggestions for ways of being that you can start acting on right now.

To use the chart, complete the following phrase for each of your goals:

I believe that achieving ____________ will make me feel ____________.

Now take the word you put in the second blank, and search for it on the left side of the chart below (i.e. if you think winning first place will make you feel appreciated, then find "appreciation" below.). Then find the corresponding unconditional way of being on the right side.

Got it?

What You Think You Lack	**Unconditional Way of Being**
Love	self-loving, receptive
Appreciation	grateful, confident
Validation	self-compassionate, self-accepting, empower-ing
Importance	connected, a leader, caring and/or generous
Belonging	inclusive, happy
Acceptance	accepting, self-expressed
Forgiveness	forgiving, compassionate and/or understand-ing
Prosperity	grateful
Fame	generous, self-accepting, self-expressed
Understanding	understanding, honest
Approval	confident, trusting

Now ask yourself: What would it be like if I gave myself permission to be those right column ways of being right now? How would I act differently if I were being those ways?

For example, if you think you need to be seen as more important at work before you can be happy and grateful for your job, then ask yourself what it would be like to be happy and grateful regardless of others' opinions. What new actions would you take? How would that alter your view of yourself to be that way?

Make a list of actions that you could take if you started embodying your desired unconditional way of being. What actions would you take if you were being generous, for instance? How would you live differently if you were being self-loving and accepting?

Here's a personal example: I almost stopped midway through launching my business to go back and get a master's degree. I didn't know if I was a good enough businesswoman to succeed without one. I was afraid of failing and I felt vulnerable. But the validation I would get from a master's degree would give me permission to trust myself enough to launch my business, right? I needed another accomplishment in order to validate my right to take such a bold risk.

But then I realized that achieving a master's degree would only be a band-aid: it would conveniently distract me from having to take the risk of launching my business for a few years. Then, once I earned the degree, the euphoria of achievement would only last a little while and then I'd be right back to feeling not good enough and not trusting myself. Earning a master's degree wouldn't fundamentally alter me. It wouldn't heal my core sense of unworthiness.

Instead, what I needed was to give myself the permission to trust myself and be confident and vulnerable. Once I did this, the need for the master's degree fell away. I realized that I didn't need the degree in order to do what I really wanted to do. The part of me that wanted the degree was the part of me that thought I needed outside validation in order to be who I want to be. The part of me that thought it was dependent upon accomplishments for its survival. The part of me that didn't know my intrinsic worth.

When we think that we are dependent upon validation, we are slaves to it. We are imprisoned by the need to accomplish, rather than inspired by the desire to give our gifts. We are in a mindset of scarcity, thinking that we need to consistently acquire validation from the outside world in order to be happy. We live in survival mode, constantly afraid of losing our sources of validation.

We can free ourselves from this imprisonment when we identify what way we want to be, and give ourselves permission to be that way regardless of conditions. In doing so, we shift to a mindset of abundance where we are free from dependency on accomplishments.

No One Else Can Feel it for You, Only You Can Let it In

When I was in 8th grade, we had to run a timed mile.

It was 95 degrees outside, and I had never run before in my life. I got four laps into the 16-lap mile when the feeling of physical nausea and mental panic descended.

As the vomit was rising in my throat, the voices in my head were screaming at me—saying that if I stopped, I was a failure. I forced myself to finish the mile, behind the majority of my class, and then I promptly vomited. In that moment, I decided that I wasn't a good enough runner to run.

In the following years, I took up yoga, zumba, hiking, kick-boxing, weight training, and pilates—but not running. Never running. I felt I wasn't "allowed" to run, unless I was certain that I could do it fast enough and well enough. I was jealous of my friends who were runners.

And then one day, when I was 19, I was in South America and I didn't have access to a gym, a mountain, or exercise classes, but I wanted the endorphins of physical activity. I begrudgingly borrowed sneakers and set out on a run around the city.

I ran through the shopping district and through quaint little neighborhoods. I ran by the water as the sun was setting. I stepped over sleeping dogs who were tied to light posts by their owners in nearby restaurants. I dodged teenagers skateboarding down the sidewalk. I began smiling at everyone I passed—I felt part of their world for a brief moment. I began to feel more a part of the city and involved in my surroundings.

I loved it so much that I didn't even realize what pace I ran at. I realized that I'm allowed to enjoy running, even if I'm terrible at it. That I don't have to prove anything by running. That I can run for the hell of it. That I was a runner simply because I ran.

Now, I run half-marathons. Not to be better than anyone or add another accomplishment to my belt, but simply because I like to run.

I sometimes still feel that rising sensation of nausea when I run, but I allow myself to stop or slow down and I don't make that mean anything about how strong or determined I am.

I don't only get fulfillment from running in the moment that I cross the finish line, but all along the way.

I no longer use running to prove anything to anyone, but just as an opportunity to be grateful for my body's ability to move through the world. I never use running as self-punishment, but as a loving practice to expand my awareness of my surroundings.

I sometimes run slower than I think I should, but I don't pay mind to judgements about what running should be like. I stay connected to the feelings in my body as I run rather than trying to conquer them.

Truth is, most of my 8th grade class would still outrun me. So, while I haven't yet achieved an 8-minute mile, I have learned to honor my body, release comparison and self-judgement and accept wherever I'm at.

When we give ourselves permission to enjoy even the things we suck at, we open ourselves to a world of new experiences.

I've realized that there are two types of people who run (and, more broadly, two types of people who achieve). There are the people who run because they think they have something to prove, and the people who run who know they have nothing to prove.

The former are the ones who burn themselves out and end up hating running. The latter are the ones who run for life, and enjoy every moment of it.

Setting intrinsically fulfilling goals

Most people set goals because they are deluded into thinking that achieving the goal will alter how they feel about themselves.

But it's an illusion to think that achieving goals MAKES us more confident or happier. In reality, we achieve a goal AND THEN we give ourselves permission to be confident and happier. The two aren't actually connected. We don't need the goal in order to feel that way—we just act like we do.

Call the goal you are working on back into mind. Recall what way of being you think the achievement of that goal is going to give you, and give yourself permission to feel that now.

Maybe deep down you believe that becoming famous will make others respect you. If that's the case, then ask yourself: "What would it look like for me to start respecting myself more right now?" Or maybe you think that having a six pack will make you feel proud. If so, ask yourself: "What would it look like for me to start being proud of myself now?"

Typically, the thing you're seeking in the goal is exactly the thing you need to give yourself. The belief that this external achievement will complete you is an illusion. Whatever feeling or way of being you think is missing from the outside is the very thing that you are withholding from yourself.

We tend to believe that once others feel a certain way about us, we will feel that way about ourselves. But the truth is (cue Natasha Bedingfield) no one else can feel it for you. Only you can let it in.

Good You vs. Bad You

As I mentioned earlier, I used to be a secret mermaid.

I wore a purple mermaid top and shimmery turquoise "fin" under my clothes to school each day.

My secret mermaid-ness gave me a sense of unshakable importance. It was like I had magical powers that only I knew about. When other kids were mean to me or I got yelled at by the teacher, it didn't matter. I knew how special I was and they didn't.

This was before I ever decided that there was anything wrong with me, so I had a deep inner knowing of my own worth.

We all have this "before" picture—a time in our lives, however brief, before we decided that there are bad parts of ourselves.

So think back to your own before picture. That time when you thought you were good enough. There was no good part of you or bad part of you. You were whole. There was nothing to hide. Nothing to prove.

Imagine yourself at that age. How did you see the world? How did you express yourself? What did play-time feel like? How did it feel to see yourself as wholly good?

Now, can you remember when you first decided that you needed to cover up not being good enough? When you decided that there was part of you that was bad, unwanted, not allowed, unworthy?

If not, this exercise might help (visit the *online resource guide* on page 132 for the exercise as an audio guided meditation):

Imagine that you have a huge picture book in your lap, filled with images of you at this age. In your mind's eye, begin flipping through this picture book of memories. Each time you turn the page, see yourself pictured in a new memory, getting a little older.

With each picture, remember how you felt about yourself at that time.

Keep scanning through your memory banks until you reach a time in your life when your perspective on yourself changed. When you began to forget that your worth was intrinsic, and instead began believing that you needed to prove yourself.

When did life stop being playful? When did you stop freely giving and receiving love?

When was that?

What happened that made you decide that there is something unworthy about you?

If you can't identify the specific incident, that's okay. It's only necessary to recognize that you didn't always believe you needed to prove your worth. That was something that you decided at some point in your past, in a moment when you felt unworthy.

This decision fractured you and caused you to turn against yourself. You began a war of good versus bad within yourself. You decided that you weren't wholly good and that you would need to work tirelessly to punish the bad within you through achieving, and hopefully earn the right to feel good enough again.

You broke yourself into two: the part that isn't good enough, and the part that would need to work to cover that up. The part that feels not good enough is the part that got hurt in the past—when you faced rejection, felt ashamed or betrayed, wanted love and couldn't get it, or failed to belong or to get validation.

Your survival instincts kicked in and told you that it is better to numb this part of yourself than to allow yourself to get hurt again. The good part began trying to conquer the unworthy part through achievement. You began to suppress any desires or needs that threatened your ability to achieve and thereby prove your worth. You began to cut yourself off from feeling fully alive. You switched into survival mode.

I remember first deciding that I wasn't good enough after I was assaulted. I thought that it was my fault, so I decided that I needed to work really hard to protect the world from finding out that I was secretly a bad girl. That was the day my secret mermaid died and was replaced by an inner dictator, who reigned through obsession, perfectionism, and an eating disorder.

My eating disorder was my way of trying to kill off the part of myself that I thought was unworthy. By denying my hunger, I denied the existence of this part of myself. Because I didn't know my intrinsic worth, I became dependent upon outside validation. When good grades, awards, and leadership positions weren't enough to fulfill that need, I became dependent upon losing weight, being called beautiful, and booking modeling jobs. I suppressed my needs for nourishment, acceptance, and love because I feared that if I let myself feel these things, I would stop achieving and then people would find out that I'm not good enough.

My story is just one example of a person turning against themselves. While my story is uniquely mine, your story from good enough to not good enough likely shares the same fundamental components. My eating disorder and over-achieving were just a surface level manifestation of a universal root cause: feeling unworthy.

Maybe you numb the feelings of unworthiness with alcohol rather than dieting. Or you compensate by needing to constantly be funny or nice rather than needing to constantly be skinny. Maybe you achieve by sleeping around rather than getting good grades.

Your story is surely different. You might have decided that you aren't good enough after something as seemingly insignificant as getting picked last for softball. Or maybe it was a much more severe instance of abuse or neglect. Do not judge yourself based on the severity of what happened. And don't be frustrated if you can't pinpoint an instance. Simply begin the process of inquiry and recognize that at some point, a shift away from wholeness and worthiness occurred.

Work backwards from your goals until you reach the source of your feelings of unworthiness.

When was the first time that you decided that you're not enough on your own, and that you'd need to continually prove your worth?

For example, if you believe that you need to get a promotion in order to feel confident, then ask yourself: "When did I begin to feel insecure/unloved?"

Try filling out the sentences below.

When ____________ happened in my past, it made me feel like I'm not ____________ enough. I decided that I would need to achieve ____________ in order to prove that I AM ____________ enough. Once I've proved that, then I'll give myself permission to feel how I really want to feel, which is ___________.

If you can't identify the specific experience that caused these feelings, that's okay. It's enough for you to just notice that a past-based feeling of inadequacy is at the source of your need to achieve.

Our work now is to lay bare that vulnerable place within that does not want to be exposed—that place that has been protected by a wall of achievements for quite some time—and accept it as a valuable part of ourselves.

Only by addressing the unconscious thought processes that keep the Achievement Trap in place can we reclaim our power. As long as they remain hidden from our view, they have power over us. As long as we think we need achievements to prove our worth, we are trapped.

I know you may be feeling reluctant to challenge the driving force of your achievements. It may seem like without your achievements, you'll be a failure and a loser. Don't worry. Keep reading and I think what you'll find is that the temporary gratification of achieving is the booby prize. The real reward is in the growth opportunity that lies in challenging our need to achieve.

The Illusion of You

In Harry Potter, the "Dark Lord" Voldemort stores parts of his soul in objects called Horcruxes. He does this so that if one piece of his soul is destroyed, he will still remain alive. Every Horcrux he makes protects him further from death but also requires him to further rip his soul apart.

We can use this analogy to better understand what happens to us when we invest energy into any belief that we are inadequate.

Each time we do so, we store away some of our power and limit our sense of who we are. Like Voldemort when he creates a Horcurx, we do this out of self-protection. We think that by stifling the part of ourselves that "isn't good enough," we are protecting ourselves from further frustration or disappointment. But really, we are only fracturing ourselves into pieces.

When we challenge these beliefs, we crack them open and are awarded the power and truth that have been locked up in them. Once done successfully, we are able to freely utilize whatever energy was stored in maintaining these beliefs. We expand ourselves beyond whom we have known ourselves to be.

Just like Voldemort tried to survive by separating his soul, the ego survives by compartmentalizing "good" vs. "bad" and believing in limitation and separateness. Challenging our beliefs about our limitations threatens the ego's identity. It will fight for its life. So in order for this to work, you must first be *willing* to see yourself differently. You must be willing to experience the discomfort of challenging your ego identity. If you want to continue being right about your own limitations, then you will not be able to access another perspective.

Reclaiming your power

When we let go of the fear based beliefs that the mind holds onto to keep us caged, we unleash our power, our authenticity. We begin to discover the magic of whom we really are.

Here's an exercise that will help you crack open your own Horcurxes, so to speak, and reclaim your power. It will help you discover that no matter how true your limiting beliefs seem, there is always another valid, more empowering perspective that you can take:

What do you see?

An animal, right?

What kind of animal?

Some see a bunny and some see a duck. We can support either claim.

Claim #1: It's a bunny. It's facing right. It has ears and a bunny nose.

Claim #2: It's a duck. It's facing left. It has a duck beak.

Once we see it one way, we are going to look for the evidence that supports our perspective. We aren't going to look for evidence to the contrary, because we figure that the way we see it is the way that it is.

Those who only see a bunny are absolutely certain that it's a bunny. Those who see a duck are absolutely certain that it's a duck.

In his book *On Being Certain: Believing You Are Right Even When You're Not*, neuroscientist and author Robert

A. Burton pokes holes in the common belief that we can actually determine when our thoughts are correct. He says the feeling of certainty is just a sensation that "is most likely a biologically-based, involuntary, and unconscious process that cannot be trusted as a reliable marker that we are right."

It is not true that it is a bunny or a duck. Either is simply a possible perspective that we can take. When we believe that we are right, we are limited from being able to see other interpretations. If we are fixated on seeing a duck, we won't be able to see the bunny in the image, and vice versa. We only have the opportunity to see another possible interpretation when we let go of our fixed notions of what it is.

But we are often stuck with our limited perspective because we rarely question our own certainty about our thoughts. When we think that it is a duck, we kill off the possibility of seeing the bunny.

Likewise, when we think that WE are any certain way, we limit our potential. Even our "good" beliefs about ourselves are limiting. If I think that "I am nice," I am confining myself to the box of niceness. I no longer can be firm and direct when I need to be, because I am imprisoned by the belief that I am nice.

We are born into this world with no ideas about who we are. No limiting perspective. But then we go through life like detectives trying to figure out who we are. We start to decide things about ourselves because we think that knowing what we are will make life easier. But whenever we decide something about what we are, we are deluding ourselves. We are choosing one of infinite perspectives of ourselves and then living as if we've chosen the right perspective. And then we go around collecting evidence trying to prove ourselves right. How absurd!

In the last section, you discovered that in your past, something happened in response to which you decided that you were not __________ enough. Because you wanted to be right about this, you began collecting evidence to support this theory about yourself. And every piece of evidence you collected strengthened your belief, making it harder and harder to see yourself any other way.

When I was little and I decided that I was bad, that is all that I could see about myself from then on. I got a B on a test—I was bad. I failed to get elected to a leadership position—I was bad. I found some fat on my body—I was bad.

I began to see my body as disgusting, because that was the only interpretation that matched my beliefs about myself. It was impossible at the time for me to see my body as healthy and beautiful, because that perspective didn't match my belief about myself.

Getting a B on a test, not being elected for a leadership position and having fat on my body did not actually mean that I was bad. I *made* them mean that in order to be right about what I decided that I was: bad.

It might seem absurd to you, but I guarantee that you do the same thing. You're convinced that you know what you are and will sacrifice your freedom, peace and happiness in order to be right about yourself.

All the decisions that you make about who you are interact to form an ego identity—a false self—that you begin to think of as your real self. You start living as if you actually are this false self. Deciding "I am __________" caused you to relate to yourself like an object. You literally objectify yourself when you decide what you are.

And because you begin to think of yourself as an object, you look to outside sources to figure out what kind of an object you are. You become dependent upon the validation of others. You want others to tell you whether you are a good-enough-thing or a not-good-enough-thing. You see accomplishments and failures as evidence that you are or are not good enough.

You have forgotten who you are. You have forgotten that you are no thing. Rather than being an infinite possibility, you are now a fixed idea. You reduce yourself to an unchangeable thing. You are no longer a person with total agency. You are a thing.

"Is" is a violent verb. It kills possibility. When we say that we and others are a certain way, we deny them the potential of being any other way. In truth, we are all optical illusions that can be seen a million different ways, none of which is THE right way. When we think we see ourselves and others as they ARE, we are trapped in the illusion.

As Wayne Dyer says, "When you change the way you look at things, the things you look at change." So rather than trying to figure out what we are and then looking for evidence to support our theory, we can invent who we are based on who we want to be, and then create the evidence to support it.

For example, as soon as someone who relates to himself as stupid considers the possibility that he is smart, he can begin to look for evidence to prove himself right. All of a sudden, he can think of many examples of his intelligence that he couldn't notice from his limited "I am stupid" perspective.

Since he realizes that it is neither objectively true that he is stupid nor objectively true that he is smart—both are just possible perspectives—he is now free to choose whatever is most empowering to him. As he relates to himself as smart, others begin to do the same, and he begins to change to reflect his newfound belief.

Turn the belief around

To have the freedom to do this, we will now question our fixed notions of ourselves.

Earlier, you filled out the belief, "I am not __________ enough."

This belief is at the source of your stress surrounding your goals. This belief is the thing that keeps you stuck in the Achievement Trap. Without this belief, your goals would be a natural form of your self-expression. They would be fun and fulfilling.

Now we are going to challenge this belief. I invite you to do this exercise even if you think that you believe that you are enough. I invite you to consider that where there is stress, there is some sense of unworthiness.

For something to be true about someone, it must pass these three tests:

1) It must be the only possible interpretation.
2) There must be absolutely no evidence to the contrary.
3) It must be true at all times and under all conditions.

So look at your statement about not being enough, and ask yourself if it passes the tests for objective reality. Ask yourself if that truth would hold up under a microscope. At the molecular level, is it true that you ARE that way?

Surely you have evidence to support your belief—just like someone who sees a duck in the optical illusion has evidence that it is a duck. But evidence does not make it true. The fact that you have failed in the past does not make it true that you are inadequate. The fact that you have been abandoned or rejected in the past does not make it true that you are not lovable enough.

Having evidence does not eliminate the potential of another possible perspective. If your belief does not pass the objective truth tests (and I've never found a person who had an objectively true belief about themselves), then that means that there is another possible perspective.

So ask yourself: "If it's not true that I'm not ______ enough, then why have I been telling myself this and acting as if it is true?"

Really sit with this question. What hidden reward does your ego get out of believing in your inadequacy? Why would you convince yourself that you're not good enough, when that is the least empowering of infinite perspectives that you could choose to take?

Why would you want to believe in your own limitation?

Is it so that you don't have to be responsible for your greatness?

Is it so that you have an excuse to not go after what you really want?

Is it so that you get to feel sorry for yourself?

Is it so that you can be right about not being enough?

Is it so that you can continue to play the victim of your wounds from the past?

You are not calling yourself out so that you can feel guilty. You are calling yourself out so that you can reclaim your power. So that you can laugh at the absurdity of the fact that you MADE UP the idea that you're not good enough.

You invented a theory about yourself and then have been limiting what is possible for you in order to prove your theory right, and to let yourself off the hook for having to be your fullest self. You've been fooling yourself into thinking there is something wrong with you so that you can keep playing small! Once you see why you've been fooling yourself, you are free.

Be very clear—believing in your inadequacy is not humble, it is deluded. It is not doing right by anyone to think that you are not good enough. It is not helping you to be a better person. It is only having you work fruitlessly to compensate for an inadequacy that doesn't exist.

The ego identity is the only beneficiary of limiting beliefs. And the ego identity serves no one. If you're ready to give up your egoic reward, then you are ready to find a more empowering perspective.

Write a journal entry responding to the following:

"Once upon a time, I knew that I was perfect and could do anything! Then one day, I got bored of knowing that I was perfect and decided that it would be more fun to pretend like there is something wrong with me. Fixing and proving myself would give me something to do! It would keep life exciting! So I made up this story about what is wrong with me:

____

____

____

____

____

____

____

____

____

____

But the tale I told myself was so interesting that I got wrapped up in it and forgot that it was a tale! I actually started to believe that there WAS something wrong with me and I forgot that I could do anything! I believed that I needed to fix what was wrong with me and prove myself to others before I could start doing what I really love! So to try to fix and prove myself, here's what I started doing:

I didn't realize it then, but it was actually really convenient for me to believe that I was "broken" and that I had to fix myself before I could do what I love (because doing what I love is risky and vulnerable!). When I was focused on fixing myself, I got to avoid or procrastinate on doing stuff like… (for example following my dream, being vulnerable, being honest, risking failure or embarrassment, going after what I really want):

Checkpoint: how are you feeling? If you're able to laugh at yourself, then you're right where you need to be. If you are not, then the tale you told yourself still seems real! If that's the case, then stop reading and take some time to ponder why you are attached to the idea that you're not good enough.

Consider that maybe—even though you haven't yet been able to see it (because your brain was too fixated on the illusion of your inadequacy)—you are absolutely adequate, good enough and perfect exactly as you are. In fact, you are unlimited.

This is not a truth (remember—there is nothing objectively true about you), but a perspective that you can take. While you do not need evidence to support this, once you choose this perspective, you will begin to see the evidence that has always been there.

Trying to look for evidence that you are good enough before you *believe* that you are good enough is like trying to look for evidence of the bunny before you believe that there could even be a bunny in the picture.

If you think you're not good enough, inadequacy is all you will be able to see, just like if I told you I was going to show you a picture of a duck, you would only see the duck. The bunny is glaring you right in the face, but when you're looking for duck, you are blind to it.

In order to shed your limiting beliefs, you must first trust in the yet unseen amazingness of who you truly are. You must trust in the limitless power of a self that you don't yet recognize as you.

All beliefs are self-fulfilling prophecies on some level. So you must first be *willing* to adopt the perspective that you are, say, an unstoppable badass here to change the world before you can begin to see the evidence to prove it.

You have to first be willing to believe that the perspective, "I am good enough just as I am. I am unlimited," is just as valid as the perspective, "I am not enough until I achieve more. I must compensate for my limitations." Only once you choose to believe in your unlimitedness and perfection can you begin to look for evidence to support it.

Once you alter your perspective, you will begin to notice that there are people who will support and love you regardless of your achievements. You will begin to notice all of the ways others are trying to give you love that you couldn't receive when you were too busy hiding the "bad" parts of you and compensating for them. You will notice that you can feel good even when you are not winning at something. You can begin to connect to the place within you that is undisturbed by external conditions.

You can begin to realize your intrinsic worth.

Most people think that they need evidence to prove whether or not they are worthy of love. But until you love someone, you cannot understand them. We can never truly know ourselves until we love ourselves. So love yourself first, and from that place of love, understand yourself.

In your journal, write down five pieces of evidence to prove that you are good enough as you are. If you can't find any evidence, you are still stuck in your illusion that you know who you are. You are still convinced that you are right about your limitations. You must first truly believe in your perfection and then find evidence to support it.

This does not only work for certain people. This exercise works for everyone, regardless of what you have done or what has been done to you in your past. Do not think that some hideous atrocity in your past exempts you from this. Absolutely every single person on this planet can be seen as perfect. Everyone is unlimited.

Believing in our inadequacy and the inadequacy of others does not help anyone get better. It only keeps people stagnant and confined to a limited perspective. Punishing ourselves and others does not give anyone the freedom to connect to their perfection, their unlimitedness, their source of love and goodness.

Until we learn to question the validity and necessity of our thoughts, we will live in reaction to them. We will use the word "is" to justify violence towards ourselves and others. Only once we realize that nothing is true can we begin to choose to take the perspective that is most empowering, loving, and freeing to ourselves and others.

As Geneen Roth writes in her book *Women Food and God*, "The realization that your internal voice does not speak the truth is like finally breaking free of your captor after years of being chained." So when the voice speaks, rather than believing it, ask yourself if you can know for certain that it is true, and if it is really helping you survive. If the answer is no, find another interpretation that is more empowering, loving, and freeing.

It is only when we are willing to challenge our perspective that we can begin to collect evidence for another possible truth.

You Won't Turn into a Monster

Hopefully you are beginning to see that the belief "I am perfect, with or without proof" is a valid perspective that is available to you at all times. But you might still be reluctant to really embody this perspective because you think that your limiting beliefs are keeping you safe and loved.

Your mind might still be telling you that believing in your unconditional, intrinsic worth is selfish and naive. Or that if you stop trying to prove yourself, you will turn you into a worthless lazy-ass. An ostracized, unlovable monster.

The voice inside you saying that? It's your big bully of a fear voice.

The moment you decided that you aren't enough was the moment your fear voice was born. It was the time when you first felt that there was something wrong with you, something that you needed to cover up in order to continue belonging and being accepted. For our ancestors, not being accepted meant getting kicked out of the village, which meant death. Evolution has not yet overridden that programming, so our bodies still respond as if we are going to die any time we think our belonging is threatened. That's why our goals feel so stressful: our bodies are subconsciously telling us that if we don't achieve them, we might die.

Your fear voice is the voice that constantly reminds you that your survival would be threatened if you didn't hide your unworthiness from the rest of the world. Your fear voice is the voice that believes that you will get eaten by a bear if people figure out that you're not perfect. Your fear voice says that if you begin to believe in your perfection, then you will stop compensating for your inadequacy and everyone will find out your dirty little secret. And then you'll die.

Often, we worship the fear voice. We never question what it is saying because it seems like it's speaking the gospel truth. But in reality, it is highly unlikely that failure to accomplish something would put us in real danger. Most of the time, the fear voice has no idea what it's talking about and certainly isn't helping us live fulfilling lives.

But before we can have power over the fear voice, we have to listen to what it's saying. Your fear voice is about to have an opportunity to fully express itself. This is not the time to filter what it's saying. This is not the time to be logical or practical.

Now is the time to let your fear voice shout its bad advice. Now is the time for you to think worst-case scenario. Now is the time for you to catastrophize. What has the fear voice been warning you might happen if you gave up your need to accomplish?

So take a moment and complete the following phrase:

My fear voice says that if I failed to accomplish ____________, then ______________ would happen.

For example, my fear voice says that if I lost my job, then my family would think I'm stupid, my boyfriend would break up with me, my friends would stop hanging out with me, I would lose all respect for myself, and probably end up homeless.

Or

My fear voice says that if I stopped taking care of everyone around me, then people would find out how secretly selfish I am, and no one would like me anymore. People would think that I'm a fraud and I would die alone.

If what you wrote sounds ridiculous, good! The first step to freedom is realizing how absurd the voice that has been running your life sounds.

The only way to get freedom from the fear voice is to let it spew its nonsense and look it straight in the face.

Our fear voices know how to convince us. They know exactly what to say to make sure we don't question their validity. Each fear voice uses different tactics to rope in its listener, but at the root of what every fear voice says is this: if you stop achieving, you'll lose love. If you fail, you'll lose love. If people find out who you really are, you'll lose love.

We begin to challenge the voice by asking ourselves: Is this true? Is it actually true that a catastrophe would occur if I stopped obsessively trying to prove my worth? Is it true that I would lose love if I failed?

Now, you might have a lot of evidence to bolster your fear voice's claims. Perhaps, for example, your parents stopped talking to you for weeks after you lost your last job. Or perhaps a boyfriend broke up with you after you gained weight. But, as we discussed in the previous chapter, just because you have evidence to support the claims of your fear voice, that does not make them true. You can't prove that it's a duck and not a bunny, nor vice versa. No matter how certain you are that that fear voice is the voice of reason, recognize that the feeling of certainty is not an accurate marker of objective truth.

So let your fear voice scream its protests, and then ask yourself: Is this really true? Will I really be in physical danger or danger of losing love, belonging or acceptance if I fail, or if I stop accomplishing?

Chances are, the answer is no. But if you have a special case where it absolutely is true that disaster will ensue if you stop achieving, then imagine that disaster unfolding. Imagine the worst case scenario playing out to its conclusion. And then ask yourself: "What would I do then?"

You will probably find that even if a worst-case scenario unfolded, there are still infinite actions that you could take to restore balance to your life. You might have to draw on your resourcefulness a bit, but you'd ultimately make it through. You'd probably be even stronger for facing the challenge.

So let your fear voice talk and tell you all about how you will lose everything if you stop stressing, hating yourself, and achieving unfulfilling goals. Resisting the fear voice will only make it scream louder. But understand that, more often than not, its warnings are unnecessary, its certainty is misleading, and its evidence is irrelevant. Recognize its absurdity and choose to act in spite of its fearful warnings about the catastrophe that would ensue. Take nothing it says at face value. Challenge every bit of its cautionary tale.

Trust in the wildness of your own heart. Trust that it does not need to be tamed, monitored or restrained by your fear voice. Allowing yourself to freely love what you love will not make you harmful or a burden to the world. Quite the opposite. It will allow you to use your unique magic in service of your highest vision. And you living your truth will give others permission to do the same.

Dressing the Wound

When people say they're afraid of snakes I'm like "you don't even know."

I am so afraid of snakes that I get nauseous when that reptile is even mentioned. I literally burst into tears when I see one outdoors.

So naturally, when my boyfriend and I were walking down the street in Santa Barbara and passed a man wearing an 8-foot-long python around his neck, I sprinted away. Noticing my fear, the man yelled after me, "He's been held by 2,000 people and never hurt anyone!"

After getting myself two blocks away, I felt safe enough to contemplate the situation. I wondered why I was still afraid of the snake, even knowing that she was completely harmless. I realized in that moment that there are two types of fear: real and imagined.

The real kind of fear is when you're on a hike and a wild rattlesnake rattles and hisses at you from three feet away. GTFO. Fast.

The imagined kind of fear is the kind where there's a man with a pet snake whom he's had for 20 years, has been held by thousands of people and never harmed anyone—and you're still scared to death.

So I turned back around. I asked to hold the snake. As he draped her around my neck, I witnessed the experience of fear in my body—how it got more and less intense as the snake moved in different ways. And I kept telling myself that she wasn't going to hurt me.

My mind began to relax as it realized I was not in real danger, and the sensations subsided. Eventually, I didn't even want to give the snake back to the man.

I committed to myself that, in the face of fear, I would always ask myself whether it is real or imagined. If it's imagined, I promised to follow the fear and do the damn thing anyway.

Fear is not always stop sign. Often, it's a green light! An imagined fear is simply the fear of the unknown, which is where the greatest exploration takes place. It's a growth opportunity. A chance to experience what's beyond it. I believe that we're one step closer to our dreams every time we choose to follow our fear.

I tell you this because this is the part in the book where I ask you to do something you're probably not going to like. I'm going to ask you to actually address your root feelings of unworthiness, which requires sitting with uncomfortable sensations.

We often avoid uncomfortable sensations because our subconscious minds interpret them as dangerous. So instead, we stuff them down and spend our lives running from having to actually feel them. But like the harmless pet snake, these sensations may seem scary, but they are not going to hurt you.

WARNING: do not just read through this chapter and then go right onto the next one. It is imperative that you actually put the book down and do this work before continuing—even if you believe that you don't need this. Actually do the work—don't let finishing this book become just another accomplishment. If you feel confronted while doing the work in this chapter, then you're doing it correctly!

Sitting with your feelings of inadequacy is a bit like dressing the wound of a wild animal. When you attempt to get to the wound to treat it, the animal will bite and snarl because it thinks that it will hurt when you touch the wound. The animal is trying hard to protect itself from discomfort. What the animal does not understand is that it will feel much better once the wound is healed, and it can't be healed without first being touched.

Likewise, when you get too close to your feelings of inadequacy, you may want to run away from the discomfort. But moving through the discomfort is the only way to heal the root cause.

To make peace with the feelings that fester underneath our need to achieve, we have to witness them fully. We have to call them out of their thick-walled cave and let ourselves experience them. We have to stop avoiding, resisting, compensating, and numbing for long enough to allow those feelings to surface.

So create a situation for yourself in which you are sure to experience the panic of not doing enough. A situation in which your fear voice will scream in protest.

It's one thing to understand that our fear voice doesn't speak the truth. It's another thing entirely to experience what it's like to not obey it.

Take an action that your fear voice would normally forbid (call out of work, tell your friend you can't help her, eat cookies, take a day to do nothing, confess something you've been hiding, admit a weakness).

Do the opposite of what the fear voice says you should do. Do whatever you need to do to awaken the voice that tells you that you're not doing enough—to awaken the discomfort of feeling unworthy.

And then simply watch yourself.

You might feel panicky. You might feel the need to compensate for your "slacking." You might get fidgety. You might feel remorse, feel guilty, feel insecure. You might get hot inside. You might feel restless.

In the past, as soon as you have started to feel this way, you have likely tried to fix it by achieving. You have probably labeled these feelings as bad and tried to avoid them by taking on a new assignment at work, cleaning your house, starting a new diet, going for a run, offering to help someone. But you weren't choosing those things from a place of inspiration, you were punishing yourself. You were automatically reacting to the discomfort. Your sensations had complete power over you.

So now, rather than identifying with these emotions, simply watch them like you would watch a storm go by. And if you notice that you are judging yourself for feeling this way, just watch those thoughts too. Pretend that you're doing a science experiment, and you need to carefully monitor the reaction that your mind and body are having to not achieving. As a scientist, you are totally unbiased. You are not judging any phenomena as good or bad. You are simply noticing everything.

Remember, it is not you that is reacting this way. It's simply your survival mechanisms doing their thing. It's your ego identity trying to survive.

If taking a day off is out of the question at this point, then just take some time to do nothing.

If during this time you begin to start planning for the future, then take mental note of that too. Recognize that your mind is trying to escape into the future in order to avoid having to sit with yourself in the present. Gently bring yourself back to the moment and continue noticing what's going on.

Now, begin to send love to whatever is arising in your experience. Send acceptance, love, and forgiveness to the discomfort. Recognize that the part of you that is panicking is the part of you that was hurt in the past and wants to prevent that from happening ever again. Rather than running from the fear, love it as you would a scared child. Rather than trying to avoid the sensations, let yourself feel them fully. Rather than numbing them, turn up the intensity of them by tuning into them more fully. Love whatever arises in your experience.

Remember: it's your resistance to these feelings that keeps you trapped in a need to achieve. Because your ancestral programming thinks that these feelings will kill you, you have been burning yourself out trying to run from them. But they cannot hurt you. You are meant to feel them. To listen to them. To love yourself through them. So surrender all resistance and feel what it really feels like.

When you are afraid to feel what's going on inside of you, you are divided against yourself. You are imprisoned by your own internal resistance. You are separate from yourself. Come back to yourself and feel what it really feels like to be fully alive—discomfort and all.

Visit the *online resource guide* on page 132 for more videos around dealing powerfully with fear.

Time Traveling

An old Buddhist parable speaks of a man who gets drunk and falls asleep at a friend's house. The friend has to leave for work the next morning, and, out of concern for the well-being of his guest, ties a precious jewel onto the inside of his clothing. The friend awakens a short while later, and, unaware of the treasure he bears, travels to another country where he labors day in and day out in order to meet his needs.

Years later, he runs into his friend who exclaims "Sir, how is it you have come to this for the sake of food and clothing? Wishing you to be in comfort and able to satisfy all your five senses, I formerly tied a priceless jewel within your garment. Now as of old it is present there and you in ignorance are slaving and worrying to keep yourself alive. How little you have understood! Go you now and exchange that jewel for what you need and do whatever you will, free from all poverty and shortage."

The ignorant man with the jewel who slaves away unnecessarily is like us. Unaware of how utterly worthy and perfect we are, we desperately quest after something that we've already and always had.

The jewel is within us. And at one point in time, we knew about the jewel. We knew how irrevocably worthy we were.

And then we went through a process of forgetting about the jewel, and beginning to believe that we aren't enough and we don't already have everything we need.

When did you forget?

It's time to go back in time to the moment when you first decided that there was something wrong with you, something that you'd need to cover up with achievement. Earlier, you identified a time when you decided that you weren't enough on your own, and that you'd need to continually prove your worth to cover that up. You are going to go back in time to watch yourself making this decision.

Set aside some time where you can sit quietly by yourself. If you can't do that right now, then bookmark this and come back to it when you can. This step is really important.

When you have some time alone, close your eyes and imagine a moment when the younger version of you decided that there was something wrong with her. Picture yourself in that moment when you felt ashamed, afraid, like a failure, or disappointed with yourself. Watch the scene unfold with as much vivid detail as possible. Imagine what you might have been feeling, seeing, thinking, smelling, hearing and doing. If you can't remember details, then invent them. Watch the event unfold and experience what it felt like to be you in that moment.

Now watch the event unfold again, but this time, it will be from the perspective of the present-you observing your younger self. Imagine that present-you is observing past-you as she goes through this experience. Watch yourself with as much compassion and empathy as possible. Having read this book, you know far more about what is really going on for that younger version of yourself than you could have then.

In your mind's eye, slowly approach your younger self and tell her what you wish someone had told you at the time. Tell her that it's okay to have done what she did and to be feeling how she's feeling. Tell her that she's not bad or wrong. Tell her that she is perfect as she is, and that there is nothing that she needs to hide or be ashamed of.

Embrace the younger-you and send her as much warmth and compassion as you can muster. Forgive her. Accept her. Comfort her. Tell her that you will not reject her, ignore her, numb her or avoid her any longer. That you will listen to what she has to say and respect her fears, insecurities and doubts. Welcome her back into yourself as a crucial part of your wholeness. Embrace that part of you with compassion, wisdom, understanding and kindness.

Now, repeat this exercise for memories of other times that you decided you would need to cover up not being good enough.

This is an exercise of welcoming back into yourself the parts of you that you rejected or abandoned. Only by witnessing these experiences with equanimity—rather than trying to compensate for them, blocking out or trying to change them—can you reclaim power from them. Only by embracing these younger versions of yourself fully can you begin to create from a place of wholeness.

Check in with yourself. Does your need to achieve still have power over you? Is there anything you still feel that you HAVE to do in order to prove your worth? If so, ask yourself when you decided that you would need to achieve this thing in order to cover up an inadequacy. Then repeat this step until the need to achieve loses its power over you.

Until we are able to actually address the feeling of inadequacy, we will continue to seek redress through achievement, and it will always evade us.

Visit the "Freedom Worksheet" on the *online resource guide* on page 132 for an additional worksheet to help you with this.

Stop Being Dissatisfied

So now that you understand that you have nothing to prove, that there's no such thing as "good enough," that accomplishments won't make you feel the way you want to, that there is no "bad" part of you, that there is actually nothing true about who you are, that giving up the need to achieve won't turn you into a monster, that your feelings can't hurt you, and that you're not who you think you are (WHEW!!), it's time to understand that BEING UPSET WITH YOURSELF ISN'T HELPFUL!

Maybe you think that you already know that but... have you ever said something like this?

"My fear of gaining weight keeps me motivated to exercise."

"The guilt I feel about not having accomplished enough keeps me going."

"The shame I have about not being in a relationship keeps me looking for the right person."

"My jealousy makes me work harder."

I hear these beliefs all the GD time from clients when we first start working together.

What they're really saying is:

It is necessary for me to be upset with my current conditions in order for me to be motivated to create what I want.

Dissatisfaction and negative self-talk are motivating.

Fear is the best creative force.

I call it struggle defensiveness: the act of insisting that life has to be hard, because you don't want to admit your ego's part in creating struggle to overcome.

I cringe when I hear these beliefs because I know that they keep people creating from a low level frequency.

I wish I could stick a straw into collective consciousness and suck-out all of that fear-based programming and replace them with these beliefs:

The more joyful I am, the more effective I am.

Dissatisfaction doesn't motivate me as much as gratitude and inspiration.

I do not need to feel guilty for experiencing ease.

I do not need to be afraid that being too content will lead to stagnation.

According to Esther Hicks (I'm not so sure about the channeling entities thing, but what she says is dope), emotions are an indication of your vibration.

From higher vibration to lower vibration, emotions go something like this:

Joy and love
Happiness
Optimism
Worry

Anger
Jealousy
Guilt
Insecurity
Shame
Fear

As you go up the scale, you come into greater and greater alignment with who you really are.

This greater alignment leads to greater ease in bringing our intentions into reality.

The higher emotional state you reside in, the less force you need to use in order to accomplish what you want.

Yes, anger, insecurity, jealousy, and guilt are motivating in the sense that going from guilt to anger, for example, would be a step up.

But just because anger is MORE motivating than guilt doesn't mean that anger is inherently motivating.

It is still much less motivating than happiness.

So while it may be necessary for us to move THROUGH these lower-level emotions, we often start believing that we have to stay there.

We become attached to these emotions because we think they help us to be productive.

We've falsely correlated shame, fear, guilt, jealousy, anger, and worry with the ability to create what we want because we have been taught to believe that joy, love, happiness, and optimism are naive and inherently unproductive. We have been taught to equate "hard work" with our value as a person.

Really, joy and love amplify the rate at which we can manifest while lowering the effort required.

Trying to create from low-level emotions is like turning the treadmill incline all the way up: making it so much harder for ourselves.

But the ego loves creating struggle so that it has something to overcome and can use to validate itself.

So it tells us that we have to channel insecurity, anger, guilt, and shame in order to have the discipline to do the hard work of creating better circumstances. It tells us that joy, happiness and optimism will be inversely correlated to our ability to produce better results.

It's like believing that we have to kick the dog in order to get her to behave.

This belief keeps us magnetized towards these low level emotions and prevent us from moving up the emotional scale.

So we need to re-define the way we think about discipline.

When we usually think about discipline, we call to mind some degree of masochistic self-punishment.

But really, discipline comes from the root word "disciple"—to be lovingly devoted to something. When you are connected to your source of inspiration, you will be endlessly devoted to your commitments.

You will find your wellspring of love, the source of all effective action, and will never run out of fuel. All you need to keep you going is a beautiful vision for the world that you are authentically inspired by. Here's the quick coaching on following your heart:

https://www.youtube.com/watch?v=ZJdfm-kNFX-A&t=69s

If a commitment hasn't come out of love, then it's not a commitment, it's an ego desire. It's something your ego thinks you need in order to be validated.

Every authentic commitment boils down to this: wanting to love, be loved, or expand another's capacity to love.

And love can't come from anything but love.

So we need to remind ourselves that shame does not lead to happiness. That fear does not lead to abundance. That guilt does not lead to acceptance. That dissatisfaction does not lead to motivation.

We need to give up the notion that we need to stay upset in order to stay focused.

We need to remind ourselves that there is a world of a difference between "my life is wrong and I have to fix it!" and "my life is already perfect AND I desire to create new circumstances because I love creating."

Repeat after me: it is never necessary for me to be upset with myself and where I'm at in order for me to be motivated to create what I want.

Completely give up the idea that the harder you are on yourself, the better results you will produce.

Find a vision for the world that inspires you and then live in alignment with that.

No negative self-talk necessary. No shame. No self-judgements. No self-inflicted punishments.

Just an inspiring vision.

The Only Choice That Matters

Now that you've progressed so wonderfully far on this path of causing your own freedom, I'm about to give you two options from which to choose. You must pick one or the other. There is no middle option, no maybes, no compromise.

Option One: You get to have your idea of the perfect life. This means that you get to have your version of the perfect body, perfect partner, perfect job, perfect income, perfect everything. You get a magic wand with which to design how your life will look down to every single detail.

Option Two: You get to be unconditionally peaceful and have unconditional self-love. No matter what your body looks like, no matter how much money you are making, no matter how well-known or well-liked you are, no matter how much you fail or how often you are rejected. You are peaceful regardless of external circumstances.

More often than not, people choose Option One. If you chose this option, then what you might have missed is that there is no guarantee that you will be happy or at peace. The fact that your life looks perfect to you does not guarantee how you will feel about it.

In fact, you might have designed your "perfect" life in an attempt to compensate for not feeling good enough. This sense of unworthiness will not go away just because your circumstances have changed. You will be stuck with persistent dissatisfaction, despite achieving outward perfection.

When I had my eating disorder, I was under the illusion that once I achieved my perfect weight, peace and happiness would follow. I thought that I would finally give myself permission to be all the things I wanted to be and live the life that I wanted to live. But as I lost more and more weight and got less and less peaceful and happy, I came to a rude awakening: external conditions are not automatically correlated with happiness and peace.

I believe that the only reason that someone would choose Option One is because they believe that perfect conditions guarantee perfect peace, which isn't the case. People choose Option One because they fundamentally don't believe that peace can exist independent of conditions. They think that peace is the result of effectively manipulating one's environment to be exactly what they want it to be.

But the belief that peace is condition-dependent keeps us in the Achievement Trap. Buddhism teaches us that attachment to circumstances is the root of suffering. If we believe that our life has to look a certain way in order for us to be at peace, then we reduce ourselves to our external life conditions and become dependent upon those conditions.

Having a "perfect" life would cheat you out of the opportunity to utilize your imperfection as a tool to love yourself more. The way that we experience growth is by witnessing ourselves through our fears, doubts, insecurities, and failures. Without these, we would be utterly stagnant. It is no challenge to accept something that is "perfect." The growth lies in our accepting the part of ourselves that we see as "imperfect."

A perfect life would rob us of the opportunity to practice self-love, compassion, acceptance, or forgiveness. Having a perfect life means that you are never required to challenge your need to prove yourself, which means maybe never discovering that there is nothing to prove, and that you are unconditionally worthy. It would mean never having to confront those feelings of unworthiness, and never truly freeing yourself from them. It would mean you may never get to truly realize who you really are.

Choosing Option One comes from a belief that objective perfection exists. That there is a right and a wrong way for life to look. That there is a certain way that we should be. But there is no such thing as perfect, and thinking that perfection exists will keep us lusting after elusive perfection, while costing ourselves peace and fulfillment.

Choosing Option One automatically prevents us from working towards Option Two. We cannot develop the ability to love ourselves unconditionally when we have total control over conditions. If we were "perfect," we would never need to love ourselves through our imperfections and insecurities. We could always just change conditions and avoid having to confront what's at the root of these insecurities. The inability to control all conditions is a gift in disguise that permits us to strengthen our ability to be at peace. We can never really know for sure if actually achieving a goal is better than not achieving it and having to learn to love ourselves anyway.

In fact, the very thing that we fear happening if we do not achieve our goal might be the very thing that we most need for our personal development. I stayed for two years at a high-paying salaried corporate job that was incredibly unfulfilling. While I knew that what I really wanted to do was inspire people, I was afraid of leaving my cushy salary and the validation I got from holding that position.

Each time I considered leaving, my fear voice shouted: "But what if you're not smart enough to run your own business? What if you go broke? What if people think that you're lazy and foolish?"

I kept myself busy with an unfulfilling job because I was afraid of having to confront those feelings of not being good enough, and of not doing enough. I wasn't so much afraid of losing the money, but of losing my corporate job as an excuse for why I didn't have to go fully after my dreams. The job was a convenient distraction from the fact that I truly could do anything that I wanted with my life.

One day, I realized that maybe the things that I feared most—having too much time on my hands, failing, going broke—would be the very things that would catalyze my growth. Maybe I needed to have too much time on my hands in order to experientially realize that I am not what I do. Maybe I needed to lose my status and my salary in order to realize who I really am underneath those things. Maybe I needed to fail in order to really deal with my fear of it. Maybe I needed to go broke in order to realize that I am worthy regardless of how much money I am making.

I realized that I was ripping myself off from potentially life-changing, perspective-shifting experiences by letting my fear prevent me from taking the leap. I wasn't doing myself any good by running from my fears. I needed to stop achieving long enough to let my fears catch up with me, so I could deal with them head on.

So I quit my job. I intentionally took myself out of my comfort zone. I intentionally took the action that my fear voice cautioned against. I intentionally caused my feelings of not being good enough to arise so that I could actually confront them and stop letting them run my life.

We free ourselves from the Achievement Trap when we stop trying to perfect ourselves and instead work to perfect our love. We alter our perspective so that we begin to see insecurities, weaknesses, fear, doubt, anger, sadness, and failures not as something to avoid, but as opportunities to love ourselves more. As opportunities to reclaim power from the belief that we are nothing more than our accomplishments.

When you choose peace over perfect, you realize that you are so much more than the conditions of your life.

And when you are free from the need to prove yourself, you can focus on giving love and sharing your gifts.

You realize that becoming famous, getting rich, climbing the corporate ladder, or losing weight are all red herrings that distract us from perfecting our love. They catch us in a trap where we are focused more on getting than giving. We think that once we get enough we'll be better equipped to give. But the more likely story is that we will be so burnt out from the rat race of getting that we don't have as much, if anything, left to give. Instead, we will need to numb ourselves in order to get more and more and more. And that numbness will be a vortex that will keep us far removed from our heart's calling.

What most of the sane humans I know really want more than anything is to love themselves and make a difference for others. We can all start doing that right now regardless of the circumstances of our lives. So rather than trying to prove your worth, focus on giving your love. Don't waste your energy fruitlessly trying to perfect yourself. The more we get caught up in trying to be perfect, the less we are able to focus on how we want to express our unique creativity and give our gifts.

You might have been caught in the Achievement Trap for so long that you don't even know how you would begin to freely express yourself and give your gifts. In the next few chapters, you are going to do exercises that will help you identify goals that are a form of your true self-expression, rather than a compensation for feelings of inadequacy.

Emotional Freedom

If we just don't take risks, don't fail, don't get embarrassed, don't get shut down, or disappointed, or rejected, then we'll always feel good, right?

If we just stay safe and never expose ourselves to the intense vulnerability of following our dreams, we'll always be happy, right?

Wrong.

One major barrier to choosing to follow our hearts is the illusion that our circumstances produce our emotional state.

It is the belief that emotional freedom comes from controlling our circumstances.

For example, many of my clients say things like, "I feel overwhelmed because I have so much to do," or "I feel anxious because I'm not sure which passion I want to pursue," or "I feel scared because there's so much at stake."

And in response, they give up on their dreams in order to clear their schedules, or they give up on their passions to avoid feeling anxious, or they choose to not take a risk because it feels scary.

Although these "I feel ______ because ______" statements seem harmless and true, framing it in this way actually allows our feelings to have power over our choices. It debilitates us from being able to really go for what we want.

What most people don't understand is that we never feel what we feel for the reason we think.

Feelings are inexplicable. Feelings are the present-tense, sensation-based language of our bodies. Feelings are immediate, instantaneously arising.

Yet the story we tell about our feelings is a whole different type of language. It is a time-based, non-immediate language. It is a language that is one degree moved from what is actually happening. There is no way to accurately and truly translate the language of our body into the time-based linguistics of our minds.

Therefore, the stories we tell about why we feel what we feel are a fiction, rooted in the past, i.e. "I'm angry because he was late." But the past can never explain the present, because the past doesn't actually exist outside of our story about it.

The present moment, where all emotion exists, is simply a dance of energy. E-motions are energy in motion. There is no true story that we can tell about it.

When we pretend like we feel afraid because we aren't certain about how to follow our dreams, we are pretending like there is a necessary correlation between uncertainty and fear.

There's not.

When we pretend like we feel overwhelmed because we have a lot to do, we are pretending like there is a necessary correlation between busy-ness and overwhelm.

There's not.

We are placing responsibility for our emotions outside of ourselves, onto circumstances.

And then we try to control the emotion to match the circumstance. We start to feel like we shouldn't be so upset about that breakup, or we should feel sadder about that loss.

Telling a story about our emotions puts them into a box, confining them to what we think we should be feeling and preventing us from just feeling the particular sensations of being alive in this moment.

To fully explain exactly why we feel what we feel in any moment, we would have to explain cause and effect all the way back to the big bang…

Ain't nobody got time for that.

So here's the trick: stop saying "I feel overwhelmed because I'm so busy," and instead say "I feel overwhelmed AND I'm so busy."

Stop saying "I'm scared because I don't know what to do." Instead, say "I'm scared AND I don't know what to do."

This allows us to accept our emotions as they are, while leaving us free to choose how to act in spite of them.

This eliminates internal resistance to our emotions and gives us the space to watch them as they dynamically move and change and morph, like clouds in the sky.

When we realize that we don't need a reason to feel what we feel, we can give our emotions space to be however they are.

When we realize that we are never happy BECAUSE we lost weight, BECAUSE we got a promotion or BECAUSE we are in a relationship, then we begin to realize that our happiness is unconditional. And we can take responsibility for it.

When we realize that we are never upset BECAUSE of what someone else did or BECAUSE of our circumstances, then we stop resenting, guilting and manipulating others for how we feel.

We don't need to explain away our emotions.

We don't need reasons to feel.

We feel happy because we feel happy.

We feel sad because we feel sad.

End of story.

So feel what you feel and go for what you want. Stop using your emotions as an excuse for holding back.

Visit the *online resource guide* on page 132 for videos about emotional freedom.

You Have Nothing to Prove

From a young age, many of us are imprinted with the belief "a person's value is based on how hard they work."

Being stressed out about how much we need to get done is weirdly comforting.

Being frantic is our cue that we are "doing enough."

But when we have free time and there are no more items on our to-do list, we panic.

Our survival response kicks in. Subconsciously, we believe that if we're not being *as productive as possible*, that we don't deserve a great life.

We have a nagging sense that if we don't constantly tread water, we'll drown.

A full to-do list is our safety blanket. The more overwhelmed we feel, the safer we feel.

We think: "If I'm not struggling, I'm wasting my potential."

We constantly ask ourselves the question: "am I doing enough?" to assess whether we ARE enough.

Whenever we fill our to-do lists in order to feel good

enough, we are like Sisyphus, damned to an eternity of useless efforts and unending frustration.

Each day, we roll the boulder of our to-do list up the hill. For a split second, when it is at the top, we can proclaim that we have indeed accomplished enough. But a moment later, we watch it roll back down to the bottom, demanding that we once again prove our worth.

"Am I doing enough?" is our eternal prison. But our freedom is not in proving that we are doing enough, but in realizing that the question itself is an illusion.

Think back to the duck/bunny optical illusion from chapter 8.

If I asked you, "what is THE animal pictured?" you could not answer me with the truth.

It is a valid perspective that it is a bunny, but it is not the truth.

It is a valid perspective that it is a duck, but it is not the truth.

We can find evidence to support either claim, but having evidence for either doesn't make it the truth because there is another equally valid perspective.

This means that the question "what is THE animal pictured here?" cannot be answered.

The act of trying to answer an unanswerable question will lead to endless frustration.

The same goes for the questions "am I doing enough?" or "am I enough?"

We have spent our lives searching for evidence that will settle the dispute once and for all.

But no amount of evidence, no amount of checked-off items on our to do list, makes it true that we are doing enough, that we are enough.

The most productive person in the world could make a case that they are not doing enough. The least productive person in the world could make a case that they are doing enough.

"Enough" and "not enough" do not exist in the realm of truth.

"I am enough," "This is enough," "I have done enough," are not the truth, but they are all valid perspectives that we can choose to take, regardless of circumstances.

Choosing enoughness is a prerequisite for living a life we love.

We cannot follow our inspiration when we are trying to prove our enoughness.

Trying to find the true answer to an unanswerable question is an eternal punishment.

When we realize that no amount of evidence can ever make it true that we have done enough, we can give up the struggle to prove ourselves.

Freedom does not come from getting the boulder to the top of the mountain, but from realizing that it is a zero-sum game.

Only then can we allow the boulder to roll away, freeing ourselves to go live a life we love.

So next time you feel the panic of not being busy enough, laugh at the futility of your quest for enoughness, declare "whatever is, is enough," and go do something you love.

Rebel Against Your Goals

If you believe that you need to change your circumstances in order to feel good about yourself, that's your clue that your self-worth is vested in things outside of yourself. This will always lead to suffering because everything outside of yourself is impermanent. It is not really you.

You are the vast, empty, infinite space in which all of your experiences arise. You are unlimited potential. You are endless possibilities.

All you are is this moment.

Whatever results you have produced or whatever things you have acquired are not who you are. They are a byproduct of who you have been being. Anything you currently have in your life is the result of how you were being in the past. For example, if you have a loving relationship currently, that is a result of you being open, loving and receptive in the past. The relationship isn't who you are.

If you think that you need to change your circumstances before you can be the person you want to be, you have it backwards. Your circumstances are a product of who you have been in the past. If you are trying to change your circumstances, you are dwelling on the past and avoiding yourself.

You are not being who you want to be right now in this moment.

If you are someone who is super successful and you identify with your achievements, it is important for you to realize that you are so much more than even your greatest achievement.

Being attached to your achievements keeps you dwelling on the past and prevents you from mastering who you are being in the present—and thus from mastering the results you will produce in the future.

When you stop using your achievements as evidence to prove that you are enough and realize that you are enough without them, you are free to create who you want to be in this moment.

When you throw out evidence of even your highest achievements, you realize that you are an even bigger space than that. You realize that you are limitless right this very second.

Maybe your greatest growth opportunity is not in achieving your goal. Maybe it is in surrendering your goal and realizing that you don't need it.

If your goal is to earn $100,000 a year, maybe going broke would give you the opportunity to reclaim power from money and realize that your worth and happiness do not depend on it.

If your goal is to lose weight, maybe you would grow more as a person instead by reclaiming power from your appearance, gaining weight, and realizing that you are not your body. Your size does not define you.

Maybe you need to do the opposite of your goal so that you can reclaim your power from external circumstances and be truly free to create from your heart.

Choose Bigger Problems

Through coaching so many dreamers and heart-centered go-getters, I have found that people often interpret their self-consciousness as a barrier to action.

They think they have to fix their insecurities before they can start being who they want to be and creating what they want to see in the world.

But all self-consciousness really means is that our consciousness, or our attention and focus, is on *ourselves*. Hence, *self*-consciousness.

It just means that we're paying more attention to what we think of as ourselves (our body, others' opinions of us, our accomplishments) than to the world around us.

And whatever we put our attention on grows. So if your attention is on your insecurities, that's what is going to grow in your awareness. You are going to find more and more things to be insecure about.

We think that we need to somehow fix ourselves before we can shift our attention to what we want to create in the world.

But there is actually nothing to fix. We don't need to get a six pack or be a millionaire before we can stop feeling self-conscious. All that is needed is a shift in focus.

We just need to take our attention off of ourselves and onto what we see is possible for the world.

When we're focused on creating a better world, our problems evaporate.

Rather than identifying who we are with external things like our bodies, our possessions or our reputation, we begin to identify more with the possibility that we see for the world—the possibility of peace, love, happiness, health, safety, non-violence, equality, connection, or self-expression for all.

How we show up in the world and the actions we take start to align with that possibility.

We become peace and our ego concerns dissolve.

We become less and less our identity and more and more a possibility.

We don't need to fix our own individual problems and insecurities before we go create positive change in the world.

We just need to put our attention on bigger, more important problems.

Because there is no escaping problems.

To live is to have problems. Solving problems is what it is to play the game of life.

So rather than having small, superficial problems like how we look, what other people think of us or how rich and famous we are, we need to start inventing problems that are truly worthy of our lives.

Problems like poverty, or domestic violence, or environmental degradation, or animal cruelty, or war, or the problem that not everyone feels loved or like they belong. Problems infinitely bigger than any one of us. Problems that affect us all.

I wrote this poem to better illustrate this concept:

"Once upon a time there was a girl who saw what's true,
She saw total perfection in herself and others too,
She lived her life just how she pleased, gave love to everything,
She'd laugh and play and dance and joke and run
and jump and sing,

One day she began to notice how others didn't live that way,
Instead of loving every moment, they just made
it through each day.
She got jealous of their problems and thought that
she was missing out,
She thought 'Maybe having problems is what life is
really all about!'

She wanted a problem all her own and thought it might be fun,
Pretending something was wrong with her and fooling everyone!
'It's boring being perfect, I'll invent something I need to fix!'
Determined to find a problem, she asked her friends
which ones they'd picked.

One friend had picked the problem that
she 'wasn't smart enough,'
Another friend decided he was 'weak' and
pretended to be tough,
Another friend had picked the problem that her
'body was all wrong,'
And another one decided he was
'weird and just didn't belong.'

At first she thought, 'How clever! Their problems give
them stuff to do!'
She asked them "is it fun to pretend like your problems
all are true?'
One said 'Whatever do you mean? These problems aren't an act!
I need to fix myself because "I'm not good enough" is fact!'

She thought 'Oh no! He fooled himself into
thinking something's wrong!
He pretended so well that he forgot he's been
pretending all along!'
She said 'Don't you know no matter what you've done,
you're perfect all the same?
You made up all these problems just to make
fixing them a game!'

She saw confusion in his face—he didn't get
what she had said,
Because what was real and what was fake was
mixed up in his head!

She realized you must be very careful
when choosing a problem to invent.
Because once you get wrapped up in it,
that's how your life is spent!

She vowed to never choose a problem that made
her hate or gave her strife,
She vowed to only choose a problem that was
truly worthy of her life.
She saw the sadness in her friends and knew
there was no time to lose,
Other's not knowing they are perfect was the only
problem she would choose."

So choose a problem that you care about so much that it takes over your life. That you live and breathe to find creative solutions to that problem.

Choose a problem so important to you that your own insecurities disappear.

As Audre Lorde so beautifully writes, "When I dare to be powerful, to use my strength in the service of my vision, then it becomes less and less important whether I am afraid."

The Truth About Insecurities

As much as we try to rescue ourselves from the grip of insecurity, having insecurities is an irrevocable part of being human. If you don't have insecurities, then... you're probably a robot.

We don't actually need to get rid of all of our insecurities before we start being powerful. In fact, many insecurities have some aspect of truth. Arguing with insecurities just keeps us resisting reality and in denial.

Instead, we need to help others and ourselves understand the true purpose of insecurities so that we can see them for what they are.

Insecurities are self-preservation.

Insecurities are the buoys that keep our identity afloat. It doesn't matter how much you try to convince us that we don't need the buoys, we are not going to let go of them if we think we are going to drown without them.

Deep down in our subconscious mind, we actually believe that we will not be okay without our insecurities.

Think about it this way: the ego is to our identity what the immune system is to our health.

If a germ enters your body, your immune system kicks into high gear and produces white blood cells to fight it. When the germ is gone, everything goes back to normal.

But the body has memory cells that will immediately recognize that germ if it ever comes in contact with it again. Then the body can quickly produce antibodies to attack and eliminate the threat.

The immune system is made up of a network of cells, tissues, and organs that work together to protect the body. Similarly, the ego is made up of a network of thoughts, beliefs, and fears that work to protect the identity.

The ego is rooted in fear and self-preservation. All it wants is to maintain its beliefs about itself.

The ego wants the identity to win, to dominate, to look good in front of others, and to be safe.

An experience of failure or rejection or embarrassment or disappointment is like a germ to our identity. So the ego kicks into high gear and produces beliefs that help ensure that this disruption to the identity will never happen again.

For example, let's say you get broken up with. The ego is threatened, because it thinks that everything that happens means something about *you*.

But it doesn't want to identify with rejection—it wants to win and dominate, remember? So it has to produce something that is going to protect you from rejection happening again.

It produces a belief in your unworthiness. It thinks that if you believe that you aren't good enough to be loved, then you won't get your hopes up and be disappointed again.

Just like the body remembers the germs that harmed us in the past and secrets antibodies to preemptively protect us from them, our ego recognizes situations that harmed us in the past, and secretes beliefs about our inadequacy to preemptively protect us from taking that same risk again.

That's why all our old insecurities resurface when the ego recognizes a similarly threatening situation.

So the next time a great guy comes along, that belief surfaces to prevent you from trusting him.

You beat him to the punch. You already know that he doesn't really love you before he has to say it.

You never have to be wrong about how much someone loves you again, as long as you believe that you're not lovable.

It's a self-fulfilling prophecy. You start seeing life through the lens of this belief and create the circumstances that validate it. The ego wins.

See, insecurities are simply beliefs that justify inaction. Insecurities prevent us from taking risks and being vulnerable.

Insecurities are like a metal shield that protect us from risk.

We wouldn't carry around a metal shield if we didn't think it was protecting us from something. It's heavy.

We carry around our insecurities because we think we need their protection to help us justify not asking the guy out, or trying out for the play, or starting our business, or speaking our truth.

The reason we think we need its protection is because we think that if we fail, we ARE a failure. If we get rejected, we ARE unworthy, if we lose, we ARE a loser.

But this isn't so. Failure and rejection and loss are a necessary part of self-discovery. They are an incredible opportunity to do the inner work of releasing false identification with external validation.

Failing doesn't mean anything about who we are. Being rejected doesn't mean anything about who we are. Losing doesn't mean anything about who we are.

We are STILL pure potential, no matter how many times we fail or lose or get rejected.

We don't really go after a dream so that we can win at it and get validation. We go after a dream because it gives us endless opportunities to grow and discover who we really are.

Failure, rejection, and loss are GOOD. They help us grow. There is no use in fearing them.

Just like our immune system gets stronger as we're exposed to more germs, we get stronger as we're exposed to more failures.

Letting our insecurities shield us from risk is not doing us any good.

So while staying safe does protect our identity, that's not truly what we want when it comes down to it. A protected identity does not guarantee our growth, peace of mind, satisfaction or fulfillment. It doesn't even guarantee our safety.

The difference between the ego's defense system and our immune system is that the immune system actually does keep us healthy and safe. The ego doesn't. It creates defense mechanisms that leave us feeling isolated, misunderstood and disconnected.

So although we can't ever really escape the ego, we can learn to tune it out when we understand that our insecurities are rooted in fear, which is just False Evidence Appearing Real, and that they actually have no power over us.

We can feel insecure and still go for it. We can feel insecure and still take the risk.

When we recognize that insecurities are not an actual barrier to action, then we are able to accept the fact that we have them and still go after what we want.

We are able to let the fear voice speak but not let it control us.

You can't argue with the body and tell it not to produce antibodies, just like you can't argue with your ego and tell it not to produce insecurities. The only thing to do is to understand why it does that, let it happen, and live your life in spite of it.

You don't need to argue with your insecurities and you don't need to eliminate or fix them.

Our insecurities connect us to our humanness.

We need to accept them, honor them, and recognize their purpose.

And then take our life by the freaking horns in spite of them.

Getting the Creative Juices Flowing

Check in with yourself: is there anything left that you feel you have to achieve in order to prove that you're good enough? Is there any remaining fear that if you don't achieve X, people will find out that you're secretly unworthy? If there is, repeat Chapters 8-12 for that goal. Do this until you find that you have nothing left to prove, and you're left with total freedom to choose your goals from a place of worthiness.

When you can see your unfulfilling goals for what they are—a mask for feeling inadequate—you are free to take them or leave them. You are no longer imprisoned by the need to achieve.

Now for the big question: When you're not compensating for past-based feelings of inadequacy, what DO you really want? What goals do you want to set? If you could do *anything*, what would you do?

Now, some of us really don't know what we want anymore. We've numbed our true calling with achievement goals for so long that we can't even feel what really inspires us.

So here's an exercise to help you get back in touch with what you really want, and see what might be underneath your achievement goals.

If you accomplished all of your goals, how would you live differently? What way would you be? How would you feel? Take a minute to answer those questions.

Now, visualize yourself being and acting that way in your life now. However you see yourself being, that's your goal! If you saw yourself being confident enough to pursue your passion, that's your goal! If you saw yourself being peaceful and calm, that's your goal! Your goal is to give yourself permission for the things you think you need achievement to deserve.

There are two different types of goals: doing goals and being goals. Doing goals are focused on accomplishing something measurable, like earning $100,000 or running 15 miles.

Being goals are internal, like being trusting or being generous. They are accomplishable right now, in this moment. Being goals are not dependent on anything external, even though it sometimes seems like our circumstances dictate how we're being. But in reality, we choose how to be, and then (when we're not being responsible for our actions), we blame our circumstances. But the circumstances aren't truly the cause.

When we think that the circumstances are the cause of how we can act and feel, that's when we think we need to achieve things in order to act and feel the way we want. That's why we think we need to lose weight or get promoted or get straight A's in order to feel good about ourselves. We think the achievement comes first and then the feeling comes.

But now that you understand that you are free to be who you want to be regardless of your accomplishments, you get to choose how you want to be!

When we think that we need to accomplish our goals to feel good, then we never feel good until that fleeting moment when the goal is accomplished. And as soon as it's done, we have to create another goal to frustratingly work towards. Our fulfillment always seems like it's just around the next turn in the road of achievement, but we never get there. We never get to truly settle into being good.

But when we think first about how we want to be and act, and then pick a goal that corresponds to that, then regardless of whether the goal gets accomplished, we get to be our desired way. Our goal, then, just becomes an excuse for us to let ourselves consistently practice being how we want to be. We recognize that the real joy in achieving our goals is in how they alter who we are in the pursuit of them.

So ask yourself, who do you want to be for others? Do you want to be someone who is trusting, loving, accepting, creative, expressive, adventurous, brave, inspiring?

Write down a few possible ways of being. Then, for each way of being, write down a goal that allows you to be that way, based on what really matters to you.

Maybe your family really matters to you and you want to feel loving and accepting. Your corresponding goal, then, could be something like having a family that communicates openly and honestly.

Maybe your health really matters to you and you want to feel vibrant. Your corresponding goal, then, could be to have a body that is strong, healthy, and nourished.

Maybe art is really important to you and you want to feel creatively expressed so your goal is to open an art gallery. Maybe the economy really matters to you and you want to feel like a compassionate leader, so your goal is to be a CEO at your company—or of your own company!

The important part is that your goal should feel good to you right now. You should love who you get to be in the pursuit of your goal. In this way, you don't have to worry about whether or not your goal will be accomplished. It is accomplished in every moment that you are acting and feeling in alignment with who you want to be. Your goal is a lighthouse that guides you in the direction of how you want to feel. It's not about getting there—it's about redirecting yourself to stay on course whenever you veer off.

When you are no longer dependent on achieving goals for your self-worth, it enables you to think big! You have newfound freedom to choose goals that you may not even accomplish, because your worthiness is not on the line. You realize that the bigger your goal, the more permission you have to be the way you want to be!

If your goal is to eliminate violence from the planet, you probably are not going to accomplish that in this lifetime. When you were stuck in needing to accomplish goals to feel good about yourself, you could never choose such a lofty goal. But when you realize that whether or not you achieve it means nothing about you, you're free to choose that goal. That goal would enable you to be an incredibly powerful and loving leader!

So now, jot down a list of goals that you would achieve if you knew anything was possible for you. THINK BIG! For each goal, also write the corresponding being goal.

Don't worry about feasibility or probability. Just let yourself create. They can be absurd! You can say that you would bring back all of the extinct species on the planet, or discover another galaxy. The point is just to get the creative juices flowing! If you get stuck, consider that you're thinking from a limited view of yourself. Remember that you are unlimited and keep writing!

Choosing and Declaring

Look at this list. These are the kinds of goals that the unconstrained-you—the you who knows your own intrinsic worth—really wants. These are the kinds of goals that you want to give your life to.

Scan through the list. Look for the ones that tug on your heart. Look for the items that scream "Pick me!" Look for the goals that you really do want, but haven't allowed yourself to admit to. And now pick a few that you really do want to go after!

If you're having trouble with this, see the Overcoming Indecision video on the *online resource guide* on page 132.

Now, a goal is just a fantasy without commitment. So it's time to declare your goal and really commit yourself to it. Only by truly committing to a heart-based goal can it begin to work its magic on your life.

Complete the following sentence for each goal you picked:

I declare that I will accomplish __________ by __________ (date if applicable), because working towards this goal will allow me to be __________, which I know I'm already worthy of being.

Then, call three important people in your life and tell them about your goal. Ask them to hold you accountable for accomplishing it. Ask them to check in on you and support you.

Now, notice if you experience fear around declaring that you will accomplish this goal. This is another opportunity for you to reclaim power from your past. That fear only comes from the belief that you have to prove yourself in order to be good enough. But that's absurd because you already are—and always will be—good enough!

When you realize that you don't need accomplishments to prove your worth, you are free to go full-speed after the goal without putting your worthiness on the line. Remember that you are declaring your allegiance to this goal because it allows you to feel the ways that you want to feel while you're achieving it. NOT because you have something to prove. NOT because you'll be a failure if it doesn't happen. The important part of this is remembering that whether or not you achieve this goal means nothing about who you are.

Visit the *online resource guide* on page 132 for a goal setting worksheet.

The Failure Challenge

When I was 15 years old, a street performer on Pearl Street in Boulder, Colorado, changed my life forever.

My jaw dropped as I watched him smilingly juggle five, then six, then seven, then eight, then nine, and finally, *ten balls* in the air at once.

I was so amazed that someone of my own species could seemingly effortlessly do something so challenging. After the show, I waited for the crowd to die down so I could speak with him.

"How on Earth did you learn how to do that? It seems impossible!"

He said, "There is only one reason why I can juggle ten balls at once and you can't."

"Why's that?" I asked excitedly.

"I was willing to drop ten thousand more balls than you were."

And in that moment, my perspective on success and failure changed forever. I realized that failure is not the antithesis to success—it is the key to it.

I realized that no one is born with a natural, innate ability to get really good at something. No one is born with the "make your dreams come true" gene.

The people who succeed aren't necessarily the most talented, but rather the ones who are willing to patiently witness themselves through failure after failure after failure.

They are the ones who are committed to failing as many times as necessary.

So as you begin to pursue your heart-based goals, be sure to not make it become about proving yourself. About winning. About looking good.

If your passion is driven by a fear of failure, it will no longer be fun. It will feel like your survival depends upon your passion's success.

You'll put undue pressure on yourself to succeed. And if you're in a hurry to succeed, you'll stop yourself from failing.

You'll become satisfied with juggling three balls rather than ten—just so that you don't have to drop them anymore. Just so that you don't have to look bad.

You'll shirk risks. You'll only play small games you know you can win.

But if you change your perspective on failure, and see it as something to pursue rather than something to avoid, the fear dissipates. When you welcome failure, you are unattached to the outcome, which leaves you free to play all out, be bold, and take big risks.

When you are unafraid of failing, a whole new world of actions opens up for you to take.

Think about it this way: If your ratio of failure to success is 5:1, that's great! That means that it's your *job* to fail! You should be doing more failing than anything else!

Rather than trying to fix the ratio to factor out failure (which will never happen), why not just try to fail ten times more than you're currently failing! Make failing a game.

This is a challenge I give to many of my clients, and they always report back to me that it gave them more freedom and effectiveness in every area of life.

The ability to tolerate failure—and therefore welcome success—is a muscle that can only be strengthened through practice.

You only need two things to play this game: a whiteboard; and a willingness to look bad.

If you choose to accept, for the next 30 days of you pursuing your goal, you will count the number of times you fail—get rejected, get embarrassed, get told "no," get criticized, get embarrassed again.

The objective is to fail as many times as possible.

More than you have ever failed before.

Recognize that failure is a marker of success, and if you're not failing, then you're not taking enough risks. You're not putting yourself out there enough. You're not growing.

So aim to fail. And fail. And fail. And fail.

And then, when you do fail, watch what comes up for you.

Any discomfort you experience as a result of failure is another opportunity for you to reclaim your personal power that you have vested in your successes.

Recognize that the only reason you would feel uncomfortable as a result of failure is if you believe that you have to succeed in order to be worthy.

Use that discomfort as an opportunity to challenge that belief, question your fear voice, and remind yourself that your worthiness is not conditional.

Soon, someone telling you "no" will be just as meaningless to you as someone telling you "hello." You will recognize that in reality, both are just words. Neither means anything about you.

By the end of it, you will no longer be afraid to fail. You might even find that the more you TRY to fail, the more you succeed.

Because you are no longer attached to the outcome.

You are no longer putting pressure on your passion.

Facing the discomfort head on and loving yourself through it is like your self-love lifting weights.

The more you do it, the stronger your sense of worthiness will be.

Visit thc *online resource guide* on page 132 for a video about the Failure Challenge.

Overcoming Procrastination

In my coaching workshops, one of the first questions that I ask participants is, "Why aren't you currently producing the results you want to produce?"

Procrastination is the number one reason.

I ask them why they procrastinate and they either say it's because they're afraid of failing—thankfully for you, you don't have this problem anymore!—or that they don't want to do it.

So I ask them why they're doing something that they don't want to do.

They say because they *have* to.

But this is the illusion. This is where they are getting tripped up: they're lying to themselves.

They are pretending that they "*have*" to do something that they don't want to do.

If you're a grown adult, there is nothing that you have to do. Every single gosh darn thing that you do is because you choose to. You have free will. Unless you are in an abusive relationship, absolutely nobody is making you do anything.

To procrastinate means to delay or postpone doing something. By definition, if you are procrastinating, it means you have already chosen to do something. Sure, your choice was influenced by others, but YOU were still the one that, after considering their influence, decided to do it.

We procrastinate when we are stuck in an illusion that we are being forced to do something that we don't want to do.

So I ask participants, "Who is making you do it?"

After a bit of digging, they always identify the person, people, or group that they feel they have to please.

"I feel like I have to do well at work to please my boss."

"I feel like I have to get good grades to please my parents."

Wherever there is the perception that someone is making us do something, there is resentment.

Procrastination, for many of us, is a form of punishing those whom we think are making us do it. Avoiding doing our work is a sneaky way that we can get back at our boss for making us do something we don't want to do.

Procrastination is actually a survival response. Whenever it feels that someone is making us do something, it triggers our inborn fears of being dominated. So we procrastinate in order to avoid domination and prove "You can't make me."

But we are reacting to an imagined threat. In most cases, no one is forcing us to do anything.

We chose to. We are committed to SOMETHING or else we wouldn't be doing it in the first place. If we chose not to do it all together, then we would have nothing to procrastinate from.

When we procrastinate, we are resisting doing something that we have already chosen to do. And resisting anything—like holding a door shut when someone is trying to open it—takes a lot of effort.

So while it seems like we are taking the easy way out by procrastinating, we're actually just wasting our mental energy by resisting our own choices.

The way to transform this is to realize that there is no threat. No one is trying to dominate us. We don't have to do anything to please anyone. We have every right to sit on the couch and do absolutely nothing until our landlords kick us out.

We will no longer feel the need to procrastinate when we remember that we chose to do the thing we are procrastinating for a reason.

We have to remind ourselves of our "why" for doing it.

Everything we do has a greater purpose. And when we are connected to that purpose, it infuses itself into even the most menial of tasks.

Taking out the trash is transformed into creating a clean, safe home environment in which we can thrive.

Calling grandpa is transformed into honoring our commitment to staying connected.

Doing homework is transformed into a stepping stone for making the kind of difference we want to make in the world.

When we remind ourselves of the reason we chose to do what we are doing, we are connected to our source of inspiration. Completing the task is simply honoring our commitments.

The task doesn't seem so hard anymore. There is nothing to resist.

But in order to do this effectively, we have to be really clear about what we're committed to. If we're procrastinating, it's because we haven't fully chosen our commitments. We allow ourselves to remain undecided about what really matters to us, which conveniently allows us to justify dilly-dallying.

Ask yourself: What's the bigger picture of what I'm doing? Why does that inspire me?

If you don't want to be miserable, then you have two choices: realize that you're actually not committed to doing what you thought you were and decide not to complete the task altogether, or remember your reason why, focus on what you're committed to and GET. IT. DONE.

Rather than focusing on being against doing what you're doing, focus your attention on what you're FOR. Allow yourself to be pulled forward by inspiration rather than pushed from behind by perceived force.

Don't swim upstream when you don't have to.

You Are What You Love

When we create goals that are heart-based, they pull us forward effortlessly. When our goals aren't there to compensate for underlying feelings of inadequacy, we are naturally inspired to work towards them. It's not stressful or hard work. It is the only work that we want to do. Our natural gifts and talents aren't blocked by the belief that one day we'll be good enough. When a goal resonates with us, it transforms us in the present moment. It makes us come alive now. Not once we've achieved it, but right now, in the pursuit of it.

Dependency on the validation of others prevents us from speaking our truth and standing for what we believe in. It keeps us in a trap of achieving only that for which we will get the most approval. If we are unwilling to face judgment and opposition, if we are unwilling to be disliked or even hated, then we are unable to freely give our unique gifts to the world.

People like Mother Teresa, Gandhi, and MLK Jr. were so effective at creating change because they allowed their actions to be guided by the possibilities that they saw for humanity. Because their life work was not about them—it was about the difference they wanted to create for others—they were able to get out of their own way. They were free to work towards a vision of the world that inspired them, regardless of how many people disagreed with them, hated them, or thought that they were crazy.

I'd guess that they didn't stress about saving the world or proving themselves. They weren't covering up for feeling unworthy. They didn't lament having to work so hard. They were so connected to their hearts that they simply knew what to do. They were deeply connected to their own intrinsic worth, and knew that that worth was not dependent upon how much money they made, how many followers they had, whether or not they made the history books, or what their social or economic status was. Because they understood this, they were free to give love without needing reward.

When we understand our own intrinsic worth, we understand that everyone is deserving of the same respect, love, appreciation, acceptance, and forgiveness as we are. Our work is never done because we recognize that we will never run out of opportunities to give love. Everything that we do transforms into an opportunity to give love and nothing is hard work anymore. The freest people who have ever lived are those whose lives were about loving.

The most creative and accomplished people tend to be those who do not force themselves to create and accomplish, but simply create and accomplish out of love. As motivational speaker Kyle Cease says, "You are what you love, not what loves you." When you realize this, you truly have nothing left to prove. Every challenge becomes an opportunity to love yourself, others and the world more. To be more compassionate. To grow in understanding and awareness. To deepen your human experience.

Just like the destination is just an excuse for the journey, the goal is an excuse for how we want to feel and be in our lives.

The moment that we cross that finish line or get that paycheck is one singular moment that vanishes as soon as it happens. The real joy in achieving our goals is in the opportunity to be who we want to be. So it is important to choose goals that positively alter how we are in the present. That way, the reason for the goal is satisfied in every moment. We're not hanging on to the illusion that it will be satisfied once the goal is accomplished.

When we're living true to ourselves, we have nothing to prove.

There's no "in order to …"

There's no "so that one day …"

There's no imagined threat to escape, avoid, or numb.

It just feels good to go after goals for the sake of going after goals.

When we have nothing to prove, our goals become games. We don't play games to prove something about ourselves, we play them because life would be drab and boring otherwise. We don't take them too seriously because we know it doesn't mean anything about us if we win or lose.

It's like what Glinda told Dorothy at the end of her journey trying to get home along the Yellow Brick Road: that she actually had the power to get home all along. She only believed that she had to face those challenges first. She never knew it could be so simple. You too can go home to your truth, now. Don't wait to achieve a goal that may or may not ever happen.

Whoever you want to be, whatever you want to accomplish—who you are right now is enough for that. If you try to prove your worth by striving for perfection, you'll end up disappointed and will waste the precious time you could be using in the service of what really matters.

You don't have to spend another moment of your life trying to fix or prove yourself. There is nothing left for you to do but love.

And remember: anytime you feel stress around a goal, that is your internal alarm going off, reminding you that your past-based belief in your unworthiness has resurfaced and you've forgotten who you really are.

Stress is your indicator that you are believing a story about yourself that is untrue. That you are vesting power in something outside of yourself.

So be grateful whenever you catch yourself stressing about a goal, because that is a golden opportunity for you to reclaim your power from anything outside of you. That is your chance to remind yourself of who you are: pure potential with unlimited power to create.

Since you can create anything, why not create goals that feel good, that inspire and challenge you and that allow you to be a contribution?

Every time you set a goal, you are creating a game for yourself to play, so that you have an opportunity to be more of who you want to be.

A game that is easy to win is boring. The games that are the most interesting are the ones with high stakes—the ones that have a high failure rate. So pick a game at which you are bound to experience failure and give yourself a chance to grow from that experience.

Pick a game that forces you to find your edge and to expand beyond who you previously knew yourself to be.

Your goals are not obligations. You do not have to accomplish anything. You have NOTHING to prove.

Your goals are just an excuse to experience more of who you really are.

Online Resource Guide

This free *online resource guide* supplements the text with additional videos, The Achievement Trap Podcast on which I interview heart-centered entrepreneurs, worksheets, articles and more about my personal story, mission and business. http://www.brandilyntebo.com/resource-guide